A GLOSSARY OF
SEMANTICS AND PRAGMATICS

TITLES IN THE SERIES INCLUDE

A Glossary of
Semantics and Pragmatics

Alan Cruse

Edinburgh University Press

Edinburgh University Press Ltd
22 George Square, Edinburgh

Typeset in Sabon
by Norman Tilley Graphics, Northampton,
and printed and bound in Finland
by WS Bookwell

A CIP record for this book is
available from the British Library

ISBN-10 0 7486 2405 8 (hardback)
ISBN-13 978 0 7486 2405 8
ISBN-10 0 7486 2111 3 (paperback)
ISBN-13 978 0 7486 2111 8

Published with the support of the Edinburgh
University Scholarly Publishing Initiatives Fund

Contents

Acknowledgements

I am grateful to two anonymous referees for their constructive comments. Any errors are, of course, entirely my responsibility.

Introduction

Who is the Glossary for?
This Glossary was written with beginning students of linguistics in mind, typically first-year undergraduates, with little or no prior knowledge of any of the topics. However, it should also be useful for more advanced students who are beginners as far as semantics and pragmatics are concerned, especially in the early stages of a course.

What is it for?
The aim of the Glossary is to provide, in a convenient format, concise explanations of concepts likely to be encountered by beginning students in semantics and pragmatics. Entries typically give more information than is usually found in an encyclopaedia entry, but of course there is less than would be expected in a chapter or chapter section of a textbook. Some terms can be given a concise definition, but with broader topics, such as a particular theory, this is not possible, and the aim has been to indicate what sort of thing the theory is about, rather than to give an exposition that can stand on its own. The handy size of the Glossary means that it can be easily carried around and frequently referred to.

What does it cover?
The areas of language study covered in this book are those which conventionally fall under the headings of **semantics,**

pragmatics, and **semiotics**. Taken together, these correspond roughly to 'matters pertaining to meaning as conveyed through language'. There is inevitably some overlap with meaning-related aspects of neighbouring areas such as sociolinguistics and stylistics, but this has been kept to a minimum.

Semiotics: This is the study of signs in general. It covers all types of sign – visual, auditory, gestural, olfactory, and so on – whether produced by animals or humans. The entries in this book are confined to aspects of semiotics relevant to human language.

Semantics: The major division in treatments of linguistic meaning is between semantics and pragmatics (although the term *semantics* also sometimes has a general sense which covers both). Unfortunately, there are no fully agreed definitions of the two fields. But there are conventions about what semantics books usually contain and what pragmatics books usually contain. (Having said that, there seems to be a tendency these days for pragmatics to creep more and more often into semantics textbooks. It is, in fact, difficult to keep the two apart.) A very rough working distinction is that semantics is concerned with the stable meaning resources of language-as-a-system and pragmatics with the use of that system for communicating, on particular occasions and in particular contexts. But that characterisation leaves a number of disagreements unresolved.

The bulk of the content of a typical semantics textbook will fall under either **grammatical semantics** – that is, meaning conveyed by grammatical means, such as *Bill saw Pete* vs *Pete saw Bill*, or *Pete saw Bill* vs *Pete will see Bill* – or **lexical semantics**, which deals with the meanings of words. **Historical/diachronic semantics**, which deals with the ways in which meanings change over time, may also be included (but less often). Various approaches to meaning may be adopted: **formal semantics** approaches aim to explain and describe meanings using the tools of logic, **componential semantics** approaches try to account for complex meanings as being built up out of a limited number of semantic building blocks, and **cognitive semantics** approaches treat meanings as 'things in the mind', that is as concepts. All these topics are represented in the Glossary.

Pragmatics: The central topics of linguistic pragmatics are those aspects of meaning which are dependent on context. Two are of particular importance. The first type go under the name of *conversational implicature*. This refers to meanings which a speaker intends to convey, but does not explicitly express:

Pete: Coming down to the pub tonight?
Bill: I've got to finish a piece of work.

Bill's reply will normally be taken to indicate that he is not free to go to the pub, even though he does not actually say that. The second type of context-dependent meaning concerns expressions which designate different things, places, or times in the world, in different contexts: *this table*, *over there*, *last night*. The general term for identifying the things in the world that a bit of language is about is **reference**, and the mechanism whereby it is achieved, using the speaker as a reference point, is called **deixis**.

An important part of language in use, and therefore of pragmatics, is what people are actually doing with language when they speak; whether they are informing, criticising, blaming, warning, congratulating, christening a baby, and so on. This is the topic of **speech acts**. Other topics covered by pragmatics are politeness as expressed linguistically and **conversational analysis**, which deals with the way conversations are structured.

Theoretical bias

On all topics, there are a number of different theoretical

approaches, and a textbook treatment is likely to betray at least to some extent the theoretical preferences of its author. In this Glossary, an attempt has been made to be as 'ecumenical' as possible, and to include all the main theoretical approaches. Also, since interest in meaning did not begin with modern linguistics, there are a number of well-established traditional notions and terms which a beginning student may encounter. The most useful of these, too, have been included.

Using the Glossary

The amount of space given to an entry is not necessarily proportional to its importance. The fact is that the essence of some very important notions can be conveyed quite concisely, whereas some concepts, less important in themselves, need a more discursive explanation with more background information and more exemplification.

Repetition of material has been avoided, as far as possible. This means that it will frequently be necessary to follow up the links printed in bold in order to get the full benefit from an entry. An entry for X of the form 'see Y', means that X and Y are synonymous. An entry of the form 'see under Y', means that more information regarding X will be found in the entry for Y.

The annotated bibliography contains a brief guide to further reading, both of longer introductory texts which contain fuller accounts than can be given here, and of more advanced texts under the main subject divisions. There is also a list of works that are cited in the text only by the author's name.

Typographic conventions

Small capitals: For concepts.

Small capitals in square brackets: For semantic components

or features. Occasionally to show where intonational stress falls in a sentence.

Bold type: Terms in bold within an entry have their own separate entries where a full definition or further information can be found.

Italics: For citation forms when not set on a different line.

Single quotation marks: For meanings (including propositions); technical terms, and as 'scare quotes'.

Double quotation marks: For quotations from other works.

Question mark preceding a citation: For semantic oddness.

Asterisk preceding a citation: For ungrammaticality or extreme semantic abnormality.

Forward slash: Indicates words that can substitute for one another in a sentence: *She prefers white/red/rosé wine.*

A

absolute adjectives Adjectives such as *brown*, *dead*, *married*, and *striped*, which denote properties that are not normally thought of as **gradable** (that is, varying in degree), unlike **relative adjectives** such as *large*, *heavy*, *fast*, and *hot*. The interpretation of an absolute adjective is not dependent on the noun it modifies in the same way that the interpretation of a relative adjective is. For instance, if something is *a brown mouse*, then it is also *a brown animal*, and *a dead mouse* is *a dead animal*; *a large mouse*, on the other hand, is not *a large animal*.

absolute synonymy   see under **synonymy**

abstract   see under **concrete vs abstract**

accessibility   This usually concerns some piece of knowledge stored in memory, and refers to how easy it is to make it available to an on-going process, in terms of speed or cognitive effort.

achievements   see under **event-types**

accomplishments   see under **event-types**

active voice   see under **voice**

addressee   see under **speech event participants**

adjacency pairs   see under **conversational analysis**

adjectives (order and placement)   There are two main positions for adjectives, (1) as a modifier in a noun phrase (*She is wearing a red dress*) and (2) as a complement in a verb phrase (*Her new dress is red*). The first is called the 'attributive' position and the second the 'predicative' position. Prototypical adjectives, like *red*, can occur in either position, but a minority are confined to one position. For instance, *main* as in *He is our main supplier* can only occur in attributive position (**This supplier is main*), whereas *afraid*, as in *I am afraid*, is normal only in predicative position (*?I am an afraid person*). With adjectives that can occur in both positions, a subtle difference of meaning can sometimes be detected between the two uses. The attributive position has a preference for more stable properties and the predicative position for changeable properties. For instance, there is a detectable difference between *The water in that pan is hot* and *That pan has hot water*. The former suggests a temporary state, whereas the latter would be more normal if the water in the pan was kept permanently hot. When several adjectives occur together, there are restrictions on the order in which they can appear:

> Several beautiful thick old purple rugs.
> *Purple thick beautiful old several rugs.

The order seems to have a semantic basis. One proposal is that it depends on concept type (the symbol > is to be interpreted as 'precedes'):
QUANTITY > VALUE > PHYSICAL PROPERTY > AGE > COLOUR
This fits most cases, including the one above; however, it

does not provide an explanation. A more explanatory proposal is that more objective properties tend to occur closest to the noun and more subjective properties further away. This has some intuitive plausibility in cases like *horrid red wallpaper* (**red horrid wallpaper*), but it does not explain the relative ordering of, for instance, physical properties, age, and colour.

affix A grammatical element that is an integral part of a word, but is not the main meaning-bearing part (known as the 'root'). The *-ed* of *walked* and the *dis-* of *dislike* are examples. There are two important types of affix, known as 'inflectional affixes' and 'derivational affixes'. Both types can carry meaning (this is one variety of **grammatical meaning**). Typical examples of inflectional affixes in English are: the *-ed* and the *-s* of *waited* and *waits*; the *-en* of *eaten*; the *-s* of *dogs*; the *-er* of *shorter*. Inflectional affixes do not play a part in determining which **lexeme** a word represents, and differently inflected forms do not have separate entries in dictionaries. Inflectional affixes never function to change the grammatical category of a word. Typical examples of derivational affixes are: the *dis-* of *disapprove*; the *de-* of *defrost*; the *-ment* of *development*; the *-ise* of *nationalise*; the *-ish* of *yellowish*. Unlike inflectional affixes, the derivational variety do create new lexemes which are listed separately in dictionaries. They frequently function to change the grammatical category of a word, as in the case of the *-ment* of *development*.

agent, agentive   see under **functional roles**

agentive (qualia role)   see under **qualia roles**

Agreement Maxim   One of the maxims of **politeness** proposed by Leech. It is fairly straightforward (here slightly modified):

Maximise agreement with hearer.

Minimise disagreement with hearer.

The effect of this maxim is illustrated in the following:

A: Do you agree with me?

B: Yes. (slightly less polite); Absolutely. (more polite)

A: Do you agree with me?

B: No (less polite); Up to a point, but ... (more polite)

aletheutic modality   see under **modality**

ambiguity   An expression (strictly, an expression form) is said to be ambiguous if it has more than one possible distinct meaning. However, since virtually every expression can be interpreted in more than one way in some context or other, the term is usually reserved for expressions with more than one established meaning. The notion of the distinctness of meanings is also important. Consider the sentences *My best friend has just had a vasectomy* and *My best friend is pregnant*. In the first case, we will interpret *friend* as 'male friend', and in the second case as 'female friend'. However, *friend* is not normally considered to be ambiguous. The reason is that the readings do not have the right kind or degree of distinctness (sometimes called 'autonomy'). Most potentially ambiguous expressions in normal language use do not give rise to any problems of interpretation. This is because typically one of the possible interpretations fits the context better than the alternatives. The process of selection from ambiguous alternatives is known as 'disambiguation'. Truly ambiguous readings show a number of characteristic properties (2, 3, and 4 are sometimes referred to as 'ambiguity tests'):

1. In normal language use, a speaker who produces an ambiguous expression will intend only one of the interpretations and will expect the hearer to attend to that interpretation.
2. Prototypically, it is not possible to avoid choosing between the alternative readings; that is to say, there is no interpretation which is neutral between the possibilities. (For example, there is a **hyperonymic** interpretation of *friend* in *Why don't you bring a friend?* which is neutral between male and female, but there is no parallel reading of *bank* in *I'll meet you at the bank*, which is neutral between 'margin of river' and 'financial institution').
3. It is not possible to activate both meanings at the same time without producing the effect of **zeugma**.
4. Ambiguous expressions show the **identity constraint**.

The ambiguity of an utterance may be purely lexical in origin, as in *I'll meet you at the bank*, or it may be purely grammatical, as in *The chimpanzee is cooking*, and *old men and women*, or it may be both lexical and grammatical, as in the classic telegram *Ship sails today*.

amelioration   see under **semantic change**

analytic proposition   A proposition which is necessarily true (in a logical sense) by virtue of its meaning, independently of contingent facts about the world. That is to say, it is true in all possible worlds: 'All divorcees have been married at least once', 'No living mammals are liquids', 'A blind person has impaired sight' (compare **synthetic proposition**). An analytic proposition which is true purely by virtue of its logical form is known as a tautology. An example is 'Either today is Pete's birthday or it is not his birthday'.

anaphora, anaphor   An anaphor is an expression that must be interpreted via another expression (the 'antecedent'), which typically occurs earlier in the discourse. The term 'anaphora' refers to this phenomenon. In the following examples, anaphor and antecedent are in bold:

1. I saw **Pete** leaving the house. **He** must have forgotten to set the alarm.
2. Pete was driving **a blue car**. I'm pretty sure **it** wasn't insured.
3. **George Bush** arrived in London this morning. **The President** will address the Cabinet tomorrow.

This type of anaphora is called 'coreferential anaphora', because anaphor and antecedent have the same referent. In 'non-coreferential anaphora', as in *Pete shot **a pheasant**; Bill shot **one**, too*, the default interpretation is that anaphor and antecedent have different referents. In some cases, the antecedent occurs later in the discourse; this is sometimes called 'cataphora': *Before **he** locked the door, **Pete** checked that all the lights were off*. In cases of 'zero anaphora' there is no overt anaphor, but the anaphoric process is still observable. For instance in *Pete tore up the letter and threw **it** in the dustbin*, there is no overt expression of the subject of *threw*. Anaphoric expressions must be distinguished from exophoric expressions, which refer directly, rather than through antecedents:

(Woman pointing to a man) **He** was the one who snatched my bag.

animacy   A property of nouns which is reflected in the grammar of many languages. It may, for instance, determine pronominal reference, use of **classifiers**, the order of elements, the distribution of inflectional categories such as number, and so on. The basic animacy distinction is between living and non-living things, but the linguistic distinction between animate and inanimate often does not match the scientific one. For instance, in English, the pronouns *he* and *she* are prototypically reserved for living things and *it* for non-living. However, among non-human members of the animal kingdom, only domestic animals are regularly called *he* or *she*, and plants hardly ever are, although they too are living. An examination of a wide range of languages suggests that there is a universal 'scale of animacy', and that different languages draw their distinction between animate and inanimate at different points on the scale. Underlying the scale is something like perceived potency, importance, or ability to act on other things, rather than a simple possession or non-possession of life. One version of the animacy hierarchy is as follows (in order of decreasing animacy):

1st person pronoun > 2nd person pronoun > 3rd person pronoun > Human proper noun > Human common noun > Animate noun > Inanimate noun

anomaly (semantic)   We speak of semantic anomaly when interacting meanings in a grammatically well-formed expression intuitively do not 'go together' normally, as in *plastic anxiety* or *feeble hypotenuses*. Expressions like these are not necessarily uninterpretable; indeed, anomaly in a literal interpretation of an expression is often a sign that it is intended to be taken non-literally. There are several ways in which an expression may be semantically odd (including **pleonasm** and **zeugma**), but the term *anomaly* usually refers to cases where there is a conflict in domains of applicability. For instance, it is hard to see how the notion of feebleness can be associated in any meaningful way with hypotenuses. Some anomalous expressions are more anomalous than others. The least anomalous are those in which the anomaly can be cured by replacing one of the elements with a synonym: *?My favourite cactus passed away while I was on holiday*; *My favourite cactus died while I was on holiday*. Somewhat odder are cases in which the anomaly can only be cured by substituting an element with a superordinate or a co-hyponym from the same domain: *?I heard a mouse barking*; *I heard a dog/animal barking*. Oddest of all are cases in which none of these strategies effects an improvement: *feeble hypotenuses*. These three degrees of anomaly are sometimes called 'inappropriateness', 'paradox', and 'incongruity', respectively.

antagonism   Two readings of an ambiguous word are antagonistic if they cannot be activated at the same time without producing **zeugma**. (For examples, see under **zeugma**.)

antecedent   see under **anaphora**

antipodal opposites   see under **directional opposites**

antonyms, antonymy (1)   see under **oppositeness**

antonyms, antonymy (2)   Antonyms (also known as 'gradable contraries') are a variety of lexical opposite. Most antonyms are gradable adjectives, although a few, such as *love: hate*, are **stative verbs**. Typical examples are: *long: short, fast: slow, heavy: light, strong: weak, old: young, good: bad, clean: dirty, hot: cold*. Antonyms denote degrees of some variable property like length, weight, or temperature. When intensified, they move in opposite directions on the scale. Thus *very hot* and *very cold* are further apart on the scale of temperature than *hot* and *cold*. Antonyms typically have a **contrary** relationship, that is to say, denying one does not automatically assert the other, as there are degrees of the denoted property that do not fall under either term. So, for example, *X is not long* does not entail *X is short*; for the same reason, *X is neither long nor short* is not anomalous (compare **complementaries**, which have a **contradictory** relationship). The simple forms of antonyms normally have an implicitly comparative meaning. For instance, *He made a short speech* indicates a speech that was shorter than some implicit reference value for the length of speeches. Antonym pairs can be classified into subtypes with distinctive properties: see **polar antonyms, equipollent antonyms, privative antonyms, overlapping antonyms**.

apodosis   see under **protasis**

Approbation and Modesty Maxims   These are members of the set of maxims of **politeness** proposed by Leech. They form a natural pair, the former being oriented towards the hearer, and the latter towards the speaker. Leech's formulations of these maxims (slightly modified) are as follows:

Approbation Maxim:	Maximise praise of hearer.
	Minimise dispraise of hearer.
Modesty Maxim:	Minimise praise of self.
	Maximise dispraise of self.

'Dispraise' includes criticism, blame, belittlement, and so on. Otherwise, these are self-explanatory: exaggerate anything that puts the hearer in a relatively good light, and understate anything that puts the hearer in a relatively bad light; conversely, self-directed boasting is impolite and self-belittlement is polite:

A: You were brilliant!

B: Yes, wasn't I? (less polite); I was lucky. (more polite)

A: What a fool I've been!

B: Indeed. (less polite); These things happen. (more polite)

arbitrary vs iconic signs   An arbitrary sign is one whose form bears no relation of analogy or resemblance to its referent. A favourite illustrative example is provided by the words for a domestic canine in a range of languages: *dog*, *Hund* (German), *chien* (French), *it* (Turkish), *kalb* (Arabic), *cane* (Italian), *perro* (Spanish), *pes* (Czech); these all refer to the same thing, but their forms are markedly different. The majority of linguistic signs are arbitrary in this sense. This is an important 'design feature' of language. The number of ways in which linguistic signs can differ is vastly inferior to the ways in which referents can differ. The expressive power of language would be seriously restricted if all signs were required to be iconic. An iconic sign is one whose form bears some relation of analogy or resemblance to its referent. For instance, the Roman numeral *III*, is iconic in that it embodies a clear manifestation of the notion of 'threeness' in its form, whereas the Arabic numeral 3 does not, and is thus arbitrary. Onomatopoeic words, whose sounds either imitate the sounds to which they refer (*boom*, *thud*, *ping*, *screech*, etc.) or imitate the sounds made by their referents (*cuckoo*, *hoopoe*, etc.), are iconic in this sense. Most iconic signs show some degree of arbitrariness. For instance, the fact that there are three elements in the Roman numeral III is an example of iconism, but their vertical orientation (as opposed to horizontal) is arbitrary.

argument   see under **proposition**

aspect   This is a dimension of meaning relating to events (in the broad sense including states) and is thus typically associated with verbs and verbal meaning. It concerns the way events unfold through time, but unlike **tense** is not basically concerned with when the events happen. The sorts of notions which fall under this heading are: whether an event is an action, process, or state, whether it has a natural end-point, whether on a particular occasion it was completed or not, whether some sort of change occurs, whether it happens in an instant or takes time to happen, whether repeated and at what sort of interval, and so on. For particular aspectual distinctions, see **durative, event-types, punctual, perfective vs imperfective, iterative, habitual**.

associative priming   see under **semantic components**

atelic events   see under **event-types**

atomistic vs holistic theories of word meaning   An atomistic theory is founded on the assumption that it is possible to specify the meaning of every word independently of its relations to other words in the language, by showing that it is built up out of simpler meaning elements (**semantic components**) drawn from a finite list of possibilities. Holistic theories, on the other hand, maintain that the meaning of a word is determined by its relations with all the other words in the language, and therefore cannot be adequately characterised in isolation. There are several varieties of both holistic and atomistic theories. Structuralist theories are typically holistic; for examples of atomistic theory see under **lexical decomposition** and **Natural Semantic Metalanguage**.

attributive adjectives   see under **adjectives (order and placement)**

augmentative affix   An affix that affects the root meaning of the word that carries it by indicating greater size, importance, or a heightened degree of some characteristic property (often pejorative). English does not have such an affix, but Spanish, for instance, provides examples: *casa* ('house'), *casona* ('big house'); *rico* ('rich'), *ricachón* ('stinking rich'); *perro* ('dog'), *perrazo* ('big, dangerous dog'). In the case of *picaro* ('rascal', 'rogue'), the augmentative forms *picarón* and *picarazo* (and even more so *picaronazo*) indicate not greater size, but a greater degree of villainy.

auto-hyponymy   see under **lexical hierarchy**

auto-meronymy   see under **lexical hierarchy**

autonomy   An autonomous portion of the meaning of a word is one which can function independently of other meanings associated with the same word form; that is to say, in appropriate circumstances, it can behave as though the other meanings did not exist. This property is shown to the highest degree by the alternative meanings of an ambiguous word. For instance, in *I do not have an account at this bank*, the meaning 'margin of river' plays no part at all. There are various symptoms of autonomy, including **antagonism**, **identity constraint**, and independent sense relations. Cases of full ambiguity display all the symptoms; **facets** and **microsenses**, on the other hand, although they have independent sense relations, do not show antagonism and are therefore less autonomous than fully ambiguous senses.

B

back channel cues   see under **conversational analysis**

base   see under **profile and base**

basic-level concept   Concepts come in different levels of inclusiveness: ANIMAL includes DOG, CAT, ELEPHANT, and so on; DOG includes SPANIEL, COLLIE, ALSATIAN, and so on. Likewise, CUTLERY includes KNIFE, FORK and SPOON, and SPOON includes TEASPOON, TABLESPOON, SOUP SPOON. One conceptual level, known as the basic level (represented in the above examples by DOG, CAT, and ELEPHANT, and KNIFE, FORK, and SPOON), has particular psychological and communicative significance. Concepts at this level are the most frequently used for everyday interaction with the world. They come to mind most readily and are typically the earliest learned. They maximise two important properties: firstly, distinctness from neighbouring concepts; secondly, resemblance between members. Concepts at the next higher level of inclusiveness, known as the **superordinate level** (e.g. ANIMAL, BIRD, FISH, INSECT), are very different from one another, but their members have fewer shared properties; concepts at the next lower level of inclusiveness, known as the **subordinate level** (e.g. SPANIEL, COLLIE, ALSATIAN), show a high degree of property sharing, but a lower degree of distinctness. Basic-level categories are also highly informative: knowing that something belongs to a particular category allows a significant amount of information to be inferred.

basic ontological types   Various attempts have been made to classify concepts under a limited number of basic types which cannot be further reduced. There is no final agreement on what these basic types are, but the following are typical members of suggested sets:

THING (e.g. *book*), QUALITY/PROPERTY (e.g. *red*), QUANTITY (e.g. *many*), PLACE (e.g. *in the house*), TIME (e.g. *yesterday*), STATE (e.g. *be afraid*), PROCESS (e.g. *die*), ACTION (e.g. *do the dishes*), EVENT (e.g. *Pete kicked the ball*), MANNER (e.g. *quickly*).

Some of these appear to be complex (e.g. EVENT, as in *Pete kicked the ball*), but the basic notion of a complete event is irreducible.

beginner (hierarchical)   see under **lexical hierarchies**

beneficiary, benefactive   see under **functional roles**

binary features, binarism   Binary semantic features are those which come naturally in pairs, such as [MALE], [FEMALE]; [ADULT], [YOUNG]; [ANIMATE], [INANIMATE], and so on. A strong version of the doctrine of binarism holds that all semantic analysis should be carried out in terms of binary features, this being how the human mind works. However, there are many semantic fields where an analysis exclusively in terms of two-way contrasts seems artificial. Examples are the field of colour terms and the field of animal types. Less strong versions of binarism propose that there is a universal tendency to make binary distinctions, and that semantic analysis should reflect this fact wherever possible. Binary features often show **markedness**.

bleaching   see under **semantic change**

blending (conceptual)   Blending theory emerged within cognitive linguistics and is concerned with processes of

combining meanings (concepts) together in the interpretation of complex linguistic expressions. Blending theory
utilises the notion of **mental spaces**. In a typical oper-
ation of conceptual blending, four mental spaces are
involved. Two of these, known as input spaces, represent
relevant aspects of the concepts being combined; in
addition, there is a blended space, where the result of the
blending process appears, and a generic space, in which
conceptual material common to the two concepts under-
going blending is represented. One indication that blending has occurred is the presence of so-called 'emergent'
features of meaning – features observable in a combination AB which cannot be attributed to A or B separately. An example is the metaphor *That surgeon is a
butcher*, which strongly suggests that the surgeon in
question is incompetent, although this is not a conventional characteristic either of surgeons or butchers
and is thus an emergent feature. Briefly, the explanation
is that in interpreting *That surgeon is a butcher*, we extract relevant features from both the concept SURGEON
and the concept BUTCHER, and then elaborate these
on the basis of our knowledge of the world to form a
'blend'. We infer that the butcher-surgeon is incompetent
because we picture him in the operating theatre cheer-
fully wielding his instruments with the degree of delicacy
and control of a butcher tackling a carcass, and with the
same level of concern for the patient that a butcher has
for his meat.

bound variable   see under **variable**

boundedness   This means having an inherent shape or
form and a natural boundary. A test for boundedness is
whether or not a piece or portion of an entity counts as
an example of the entity. For example, if we take a bottle

of milk and pour some of it into a cup, the portion in the cup still qualifies for the label *milk* because the concept MILK does not have a natural boundary. But if we remove, say, a wheel from a car, it does not qualify for the label *a car*. The notion of boundedness also applies to events. An **accomplishment** is a bounded event (it has an inherent beginning and end), whereas an activity is unbounded. If Liz plays the first page of a piano sonata, we can describe this by saying *Liz played the piano* (activity), but we cannot say *Liz played the sonata* (accomplishment).

bystander   see under **speech event participant**

C

case   This is an inflectional category of nouns or noun-phrases. Different cases indicate different syntactic functions, such as subject, object, and complement of a verb, object of preposition, and so on, or **functional roles**, such as **agent** or **instrument**.

case roles   see **functional roles**

cataphora   see under **anaphora**

category boundaries   see under **prototype theory**

circumstantial roles   These are distinguished from the **functional roles** in a sentence by the fact that they are less central to the designated event. Expressions fulfilling circumstantial roles are typically optional, in the sense that they can be omitted without giving rise to ungrammaticality, **latency,** or a change in the meaning of the verb, any of which would indicate a functional role. The difference between circumstantial and functional roles can be illustrated as follows. Consider the sentence *Pete teaches in London*. Here, one can omit *in London* without either anomaly or change in the meaning of the verb: *Pete teaches*; hence, *in London* fulfils a circumstantial role. Contrast this with *Pete lives in London*. Omitting *in London* certainly leaves a possible sentence *Pete lives*, but not without a change in the meaning of *live* from 'dwell' to 'be alive'. This indicates that *in London* in this case represents a functional role.

classical theory of concepts (also known as the definitional theory)   According to this theory, every **concept** is associated with a definition; everything that satisfies the definition falls under the concept (that is to say, belongs to the corresponding **conceptual category**) and everything that fails to satisfy the definition is excluded. Definitions typically take the form of a set of features, or criteria, which are individually necessary for membership of the category and are jointly sufficient. Take the case of the concept BOY, which we might define as 'young male human'. These features are individually necessary, in that every member of the category BOY must be male, must be young, and must be human. The features are jointly sufficient, in that everything which possesses all three features qualifies as a boy. This approach to concepts has an intuitive appeal, but the major drawbacks are:

1. For many concepts – probably the majority – it is extremely difficult to come up with satisfactory definitions.
2. This approach implies that categories have sharp boundaries, whereas natural categories typically have **fuzzy boundaries**.

3. With this approach, everything that satisfies a definition has equal status in a category. This does not explain why, typically, some members of a category are felt to be more central and others more peripheral.

For theories which attempt to deal with one or more of these objections, see **prototype theory**, **exemplar theory**, the **'theory' theory**.

classifiers   In many languages it is not possible to count things directly, in the manner of the English *three cows*, *six books*, and so on. One must use a special grammatical element called a classifier, usually either a separate word or an affix, that encodes some semantic property of the noun being counted. So, for instance, if English had classifiers, we might say something like *three animal cows* and *six object books*. Indonesian has three commonly used classifiers, illustrated below (from Frawley):

se-	orang	mahasiswa
one	Human	student
'one student'		
se-	ekor	kuda
one	Animal	horse
'one horse'		
se-	buah	buku
one	Inanimate	book
'one book'		

Some languages have a large number of classifiers. Japanese, for instance, has separate classifiers for aeroplanes, small boats, large boats, train coaches, buildings, schools, and houses, among many others.

clausal implicatures   see under **generalised vs particularised conversational implicatures**

cliché   The definition of this in the *Longman Dictionary of the English Language* is: "a hackneyed phrase or expression". The same dictionary defines *hackneyed* as "lacking in freshness or originality; meaningless because used or done too often". The *Oxford Advanced Learner's Dictionary* gives *A trouble shared is a trouble halved* as an example of cliché. The Longman definition is curious because most of what anyone says is "lacking in freshness or originality", and furthermore, the frequent use of words like *chair*, *dog*, or *walk* does not seem to have resulted in a loss of meaning. A definition of the everyday meaning of cliché should point out (a) that it is a criticism and (b) that it applies to an expression that purports to be interesting or original. Someone who says *Sometimes when you are worried about something, it helps to talk about it* would be unlikely to be accused of using a cliché. In linguistics, the term sometimes has a different meaning. It is used to refer to a phrase that, like an **idiom**, is stored in the **mental lexicon** in a ready-made form, but, unlike an idiom, is semantically transparent. Examples are: *This is a tax-and-spend Government*, *You'll have to wait and see*.

closed set items   These are grammatical elements, either **affixes** or free words, which have three main characteristics:

1. In a grammatical sentence the possibilities of omitting or substituting them without affecting the grammaticality of the sentence are very limited or non-existent.
2. They belong to substitution sets whose membership is effectively fixed, with change occurring only over a long time-scale (typically longer than the lifetime of a single speaker).

3. Their main function is to articulate the grammatical structure of a sentence, and while most of them can be said to carry meaning, their meanings are typically basic and very general (see under **grammatical meaning**).

(Compare **open set items**.)

cognitive linguistics   An approach to the study of language structure and linguistic behaviour that has developed mainly since the 1980s. Underlying this approach are a number of basic assumptions. The first is that language has evolved for the purpose of conveying meaning, and so all its structures, whether semantic, syntactic, or phonological, should be related to this function. The second is that linguistic abilities are embedded in, and are inseparable from, general cognitive abilities, there being no autonomous portion of the brain specialised for language. A consequence of this for semantics is that no principled distinction can be drawn between linguistic meaning and general knowledge. The third assumption is that meaning is conceptual in nature and involves shaping or imposing form on conceptual and perceptual raw material in specific ways. Cognitive linguists maintain that a truth-conditional approach cannot give an adequate account of meaning. Cognitive linguistics has close links with cognitive psychology, drawing particularly on work on the structure and nature of concepts. Two scholars have been especially influential in developing this approach: Lakoff and Langacker.

coherence   see under **cohesion vs coherence**

cohesion vs coherence   These are types of connectedness which distinguish texts from random collections of words. Cohesion is a matter of form and concerns (mainly grammatical) ways of connecting one piece of language to another, such as agreement and **anaphora**. Coherence is a matter of meaning compatibility and relevance. Mini-text 1 is cohesive, but not coherent, whereas mini-text 2 is short on overt indicators of cohesion, but is coherent:

1. My father came into my room. So I plugged him in and switched him on.
2. There was a loud knock. I opened the door. Two policemen.

collective plural   see under **plural**

collocation   This term is used in two main ways. The first use refers to any grammatically well-formed sequence of words that go together without oddness, such as *an excellent performance*. We say that, for instance, *excellent* 'collocates with' *performance*, meaning that they go together normally; we can also say that *excellent* is 'a normal collocate' of *performance*. The other use is to refer to a sequence of words that is **compositional** (unlike a prototypical **idiom**, for example), but nonetheless forms a unit in some way. This may simply be because they occur together very frequently, but usually the sequence also has a semantic unity. For instance, one or more of the constituent words may have a special sense which only appears in that combination, or in a limited set of related combinations. The following expressions, for instance, are collocations in this sense: *a high wind, high seas, high office, have a high opinion of*. In each case, the word *high* has a (different) special meaning, and this meaning is different from the **default meaning** present in, for instance, *a high wall*. (This type of collocation is sometimes called an 'encoding idiom'.)

committedness (in antonyms)   see under **polar antonyms**

common ground   This refers to aspects of knowledge that participants in an act of communication assume to be shared and therefore do not need to be spelled out. It includes what can be perceived in the immediate context, together with knowledge of the language, general world knowledge, shared attitudes, and so on.

common nouns   see under **proper nouns**

comparative   see under **degrees of comparison**

competence vs performance   This distinction, made by Chomsky, is related to the distinction proposed by Saussure between **langue** and **parole**. As a first approximation, competence can be equated to langue, except that it is conceived as the neural representation of the system as it exists in the mind of an ideal speaker-hearer. Performance takes a slightly different perspective to parole, in that it refers in the first place to the processes involved in the production of utterances, rather than the produced utterances themselves.

complementarity, complementaries   Complementarity is a type of **oppositeness**. Complementary terms divide a domain into two mutually exclusive sub-domains: if something belongs to the domain, then it must fall under one or other of the terms. Complementaries have a **contradictory** relation. So, for example, if something is not *dead* it must be *alive*, and if it is not *alive* then it must be *dead*, and it is anomalous to say of an organism that it is *neither dead nor alive*. This establishes *dead* and *alive* as complementaries (compare **antonyms (2)**, which have a **contrary** relation). The complementary relationship between *dead* and *alive* only appears if what they are applied to belongs to the appropriate domain, in this case, the domain of organisms. For instance, *The table is not alive* does not entail *The table is dead*. Other examples of complementaries are: *open (adj.): shut (adj.), true: false, continue V-ing: stop V-ing*.

complements   see under **semantic heads**

compositional expressions   see under **compositionality (principle of)**

compositionality (principle of)   The principle of compositionality states that the meaning of a complex expression is a compositional function of the meanings of its parts. That is to say, we work out the meaning of an expression containing more than one meaningful element by combining the meanings of its constituents. So, to get the meaning of, say, *The cat ate the fish*, we add together the meanings of the individual items:
'The cat ate the fish' = 'the' + 'cat' + 'ate' + 'the' + 'fish'
The appropriate way of combining the meanings is given by the syntax. One way or another, this must be true in general terms otherwise we would have to learn the meanings of all multi-word expressions separately. However, not all expressions of a language conform to this principle. Those that do are described as 'compositional'; those that do not are described as 'non-compositional' or 'semantically opaque'. Semantic opacity (which is a matter of degree) is a prototypical characteristic of **idioms**.

concepts, conceptual categories   To a first approximation, conceptual categories are classes of entities in the world, like DOG, CHAIR, DICTATORSHIP (we must interpret 'entity' in the broadest sense, to include properties like

RED, actions like SPEAK, and so on). They represent the way we articulate our experience of the world to make it manageable, by dividing it into classes whose members have similar properties. Concepts, on the other hand, are mental representations that store knowledge about categories, enabling us to assign things to appropriate categories. The ability to deal with the world in terms of categories rather than individual objects, experiences, and so forth has enormous advantages:

1. Learning from experience: individual experiences rarely repeat themselves exactly, so storing information about each separate one would be of limited usefulness. If, however, we group similar objects, events, and so on into categories, then these categories do recur and can be associated with a useful build-up of knowledge.
2. Communication: language would not be able to function unless its elements were associated with shared conceptual categories.
3. Planning: concepts and their associated stored knowledge enable us to carry out a virtual manipulation of things in the world and foresee consequences.
4. Economy: what is learned about one member of a category can be instantly generalised to other members. Conversely, learning that something belongs to a particular category gives immediate access to further information about it.

There are various theories regarding the nature of concepts. See, for instance, the **classical theory**, **prototype theory**, **exemplar theory**, the **'theory' theory**. No adequate theory of meaning can ignore concepts. The most straightforward way of relating word meanings to concepts is to say that they are the same.

conceptual axiology   see **Natural Semantic Metalanguage**

Conceptual Metaphor Theory   This is a theory of metaphor developed by Lakoff. The basic idea is that metaphor is essentially a relation between conceptual domains, whereby ways of talking about one domain (the 'source domain') can be applied to another domain (the 'target domain') by virtue of 'correspondences' between the two. Typically, the source domain is relatively familiar and conceptually well-structured, and the structures are used to articulate the target domain. In the case of well-established metaphors, the correspondences are held to be permanently laid down in the cognitive system. By this theory, metaphor is not tied to particular linguistic expressions: a given conceptual metaphor can in principle underlie any number of metaphorical expressions, some of which may be conventionalised, others not. An example of a conceptual metaphor is LIFE IS A JOURNEY. Here, the source domain is that of JOURNEY and the target domain – what the metaphorical expression refers to – is that of LIFE. The following are some of the relevant correspondences between these domains:

JOURNEY	LIFE
beginning of journey	birth
end of journey	death
reaching destination	achieving aim
crossroads	point of choice
going uphill	finding life difficult
obstacles	difficulties
fellow-travellers	partners, colleagues, friends

These correspondences allow expressions such as the following to be interpreted:

My son is just beginning life's journey.

His progress has been a bit slow, but I think he's now got where he wants to be.

We've come a long way together, you and I, and we've overcome many obstacles.

She has come to a crossroads in her life.

I want to put my affairs in order: I'm getting near the end of the road.

conceptual semantics   A variety of componential semantics (see under **semantic components**) associated with the linguist Jackendoff. Jackendoff holds that meanings are essentially conceptual in nature, and that the meanings of sentences are conceptual complexes built up out of basic conceptual components. His system is particularly concerned with the mapping between syntactic structures and conceptual structures. He utilises a set of universal basic ontological categories, which includes such items as EVENT, STATE, OBJECT, PATH, PLACE, and PROPERTY. Many of these categories can be sub-divided using basic semantic features. For instance, OBJECTS (in the broad sense of 'material entities') can be sub-classified using the features [+/– INTERNAL STRUCTURE] and [+/– BOUNDED]:

count nouns: individuals
(e.g. *chair*, *dog*, *house*)
                          [+BOUNDED][–INTERNAL STRUCTURE]
collective nouns: groups
(e.g. *team*, *family*)
                          [+BOUNDED][+INTERNAL STRUCTURE]
mass nouns: substances
(e.g. *milk*, *glass*)
                          [–BOUNDED][–INTERNAL STRUCTURE]
plural nouns: aggregates
(e.g. *chairs*, *dogs*)
                          [–BOUNDED][+INTERNAL STRUCTURE]

The following example illustrates the semantic analysis of a sentence in this system:

Bill went into the house
syntactic analysis: [$_s$ [$_{NP}$ Bill] [$_{VP}$ [$_V$ went] [$_{PP}$ [$_P$ into] [$_{NP}$ the house]]]]
semantic analysis: [$_{EVENT}$ GO ([$_{THING}$ BILL], [$_{PATH}$ TO ([$_{PLACE}$ IN ([$_{THING}$ HOUSE])])])]

concrete vs abstract   Roughly speaking, *concrete* in semantics refers to whatever can be seen, heard, tasted, smelled, touched, or felt directly. Whatever has an indirect relation to sensory experience is *abstract*. So, a chair is concrete, but the rate of inflation is abstract; to kick someone is a concrete act, but to excommunicate them is an abstract act; the property of being red is concrete, but that of being illegal is abstract.

connotation   This has several different meanings:

1. In everyday language (often used in the plural) it means little more than 'associations': *For many Americans, the term 'liberal' has negative connotations.*

2. In a more technical use it refers to non-truth-conditional aspects of meaning. These may involve expressive features, such as the derogatory nature of *hovel* or *slum*, or register allegiance, such as the difference in formality between *pass away* and *kick the bucket*. They may also be features which are characteristic, but not logically necessary, like the barking of dogs.

3. It is sometimes used in a way equivalent to **intension**: the word *dog* may be said to denote the class of dogs, but connote the property of 'dogness'.

constatives   In his early work on **speech acts**, the philosopher Austin drew a distinction between constative utterances, like *The cat sat on the mat*, which had a purely descriptive (statement-making) function and which could be treated in terms of truth and falsehood, and performative utterances, like *I promise it will never happen again*, which he claimed were neither true nor false but felicitous or infelicitous. In his later work, however, Austin dropped this distinction in favour of a distinction between explicit performatives (like *I promise it will never happen again*) and primary or implicit performatives (like *It will never happen again*, functioning as a promise). Even utterances like *The cat sat on the mat* were recognised as including a performative element of 'stating'.

constitutive role   see under **qualia roles**

constraints on relevance   This notion is used by proponents of **Relevance Theory** to explain certain aspects of **nonpropositional** meaning, especially the meanings of elements such as *but* or *what's more*. Take the word *but*. Clearly, *Liz is blonde and beautiful* and *Liz is blonde but beautiful* do not mean the same. Yet they have the same **propositional content**: they are true and false in the same circumstances. Where *but* differs is in what it tells us about the relevance of what follows. It indicates that the following information contradicts some belief or assumption on the part of the hearer. In a similar spirit we can say that *what's more* indicates that what follows, in the speaker's opinion, reinforces some prior belief or opinion.

construal   This notion is crucial to the **cognitive linguistic** approach to the study of language. It is basically a cognitive act of imposing some sort of structure on a body of conceptual content, such as profiling a portion of a **domain**, or viewing something from a particular perspective. The meaning of a linguistic expression indicates (a) a domain to be activated and (b) how the domain is to be construed.

context   An essential factor in the interpretation of utterances and expressions. The most important aspects of context are: (1) preceding and following utterances and/or expressions ('co-text'), (2) the immediate physical situation, (3) the wider situation, including social and power relations, and (4) knowledge presumed shared between speaker and hearer.

contextual modulation   This refers to different interpretations of a word (in different contexts) which do not exhibit any signs of **autonomy**, and thus cannot be considered to represent different **senses**, different **facets**, or different **microsenses**. An example is the 'male friend': 'female friend' contrast observable in *My best friend has just had a vasectomy* and *My best friend is pregnant*, or the different shade of colour indicated in *blue with cold* and *blue sky*. Contextual modulations are not normally given separate treatment in dictionaries.

contextual theory of meaning   see under **atomistic vs holistic theories of word meaning**

continuous signs   see under **discrete vs continuous signs**

contradictory   Two propositions are contradictory if the truth of one entails the falsity of the other, and the falsity of one entails the truth of the other. That is to say, they cannot either both be true or both false. For instance,

'This statement is true' and 'This statement is false' are contradictory propositions. The term is also applied to lexical items related by **complementarity**.

contrary   Two propositions stand in a contrary relation to one another if the truth of one entails the falsity of the other, but the falsity of one does not entail the truth of the other. This means that they cannot both be true, but they may both be false. For instance, 'Toby is a cat' and 'Toby is a dog' are contrary propositions, because Toby cannot be both a cat and a dog, but he may be neither (e.g. a guinea pig). This relationship underlies the notion of **incompatibility** in lexical semantics, as well as some varieties of opposite, such as **polar antonyms**.

conventional implicatures   These are components of the meanings of utterances which are not propositional in nature, but which have a stable association with particular linguistic expressions and which therefore cannot be cancelled without **anomaly**. For instance, *Pete hasn't registered yet* and *Pete hasn't registered* are propositionally identical, but the presence of *yet* in the former implicates that Pete is still expected to arrive (*still* and *already* have similar properties). Contradicting this leads to oddness: *?Pete hasn't registered yet and I know for a fact he does not intend to*. Another example is the 'interrogative' aspect of the meaning of a question such as *Why are you here?*, which cannot be described as true or false and which leads to anomaly if denied: *?I don't want to know the reasons for your presence, but why are you here?*

conventional signs   see under **natural vs conventional signs**

conversational analysis   This is an area of study, nowadays usually considered a branch of pragmatics, concerned with the structure of natural conversations. The approach is strictly empirical. Actually occurring conversations are meticulously recorded and studied without theoretical preconceptions, whether semantic, philosophical, or deriving from other branches of pragmatics. The aim is to extract regularities of organisation. Only a few of the most basic notions can be mentioned here. The basic unit of description in conversational analysis is the 'turn' (sometimes called the 'turn constructional unit'). This is an uninterrupted contribution of one speaker to a conversation, followed and preceded by a change of speaker unless it represents the beginning or end of the conversation. Turns are said to be 'latched' if there is no detectable gap between the end of one turn and the beginning of the next. They may occasionally 'overlap'. A slight pause may signal a 'transition-relevance place', where the turn is offered to another participant. A speaker may start to say something, then change their mind about what to say; this is known as a 'repair'. A hearer may produce what are known as 'back channel cues', like *Yeah, hmmm, Wow!*, which are not intended to interrupt the speaker's flow, nor to take over the turn. Conversations are structured in a number of ways. For instance, certain utterances serve to initiate a conversation (e.g. *Hi!*), while others serve to terminate them (e.g. *See you later!*). Some turns form natural pairs, known as 'adjacency pairs'. Examples of these are question and answer, greeting and response greeting, invitation and acceptance or refusal, and apology and acceptance or rejection.

conversational implicatures   One of two basic types of **implicature** (the other type being **conventional implicatures**). Conversational implicatures have four main identifying features:

1. They are not **entailments**, that is, they do not
   follow logically from what is said. For instance, we
   can infer from 'Pete has a cousin' that 'At least one
   of Pete's parents is not an only child', but since this
   is an entailment it is not a conversational implicature. On the other hand, in the example given
   under implicature:

   A: Can I speak to Jane?

   B: Jane's in the shower.

   the inference from B's answer, that Jane is not able
   to take a telephone call, is not an entailment.

2. They are 'cancellable' (or 'defeasible'), that is, they
   are relatively weak inferences and can be denied by
   the speaker without contradiction. For instance, B's
   reply in the following would normally be taken to
   mean 'I don't intend to tell you':

   A: How old are you?

   B: That's none of your business.

   If B added 'But I'll tell you, anyway' this would
   cancel the inference, but B would not be guilty of
   self-contradiction. This is characteristic of conversational implicatures. In contrast, an attempt to
   cancel an entailment leads to a contradiction:

   ?Pete has a cousin, but both his parents are only
   children.

3. They are 'context sensitive', in that the same
   proposition expressed in a different context can
   give rise to different implicatures:

   A: I think I'll take a shower.

   B: Jane's in the shower.

   This implicates 'You can't take a shower just yet',
   not 'Jane can't accept a phone call'.

4. They are 'non-detachable', that is, in a particular
   context the same proposition expressed in different
   words will give rise to the same implicature. In

other words, the implicature is not tied to a particular form of words (cf. **conventional implicatures**). For instance, if B in 2 above had said 'That doesn't concern you', the implicature would be the same.

5. They are 'calculable', that is to say they can be worked out using general principles rather than requiring specific knowledge, such as a private arrangement between A and B that if one says X it will mean Y.

(See also under **generalised vs particularised conversational implicatures**.)

converse (relation)   A logical relation R' is the converse of another relation R if and only if, for any pair of **arguments** x and y, xRy and $yR'x$ are logically equivalent, that is to say they are mutually entailing. (See the next entry for illustrations of how this notion is used in semantics.)

converse (lexical)   Lexical converses are a species of opposite. Two expressions which are converses designate a given state of affairs or event from the perspective of two different participants. For instance 'A is above B' describes a spatial relationship between two entities A and B by locating A with reference to B; the same state of affairs is described by 'B is below A', but this time B is located with reference to A. The mutual **entailment** relation between 'A is above B' and 'B is below A', in which the **arguments** are reversed and *above* is replaced by *below*, establishes *above* and *below* as lexical converses. Other examples are *in front of: behind* ('A is in front of B', 'B is behind A'), *follow: precede* ('B follows A in the alphabet', 'A precedes B in the alphabet'), *parent: offspring* ('X and Y are A's parents', 'A is X and

Y's offspring'), and *buy/sell* ('A bought B from C', 'C sold B to A'). The comparative forms of adjectival opposites stand in a converse relationship ('X is longer than Y', 'Y is shorter than X'), as do the active and passive forms of transitive verbs: 'Pete built this house', 'This house was built by Pete'.

Co-operative Principle   This was suggested by the philosopher Grice as the basis for an explanation of how **conversational implicatures** arise. Grice portrayed a conversation as a co-operative activity in which participants tacitly agree to abide by certain norms. His formulation of the general principle runs as follows: "Make your conversational contribution such as is required, at the stage at which it occurs, by the accepted purpose or direction of the talk exchange in which you are engaged." Grice spelled out the norms in greater detail in the form of a set of **maxims of conversation**.

coreferential anaphora   see under **anaphora**

cost-benefit scale   see under **Tact and Generosity Maxims**

co-text   see under **context**

correspondences (metaphorical)   see under **Conceptual Metaphor Theory**

countability   Nouns are described as 'count nouns' if they occur normally in the plural, and with numerals and other expressions of 'numerousness' (*two hundred horses, several horses, a few horses*), but not with expressions of quantity such as *a little, much, a lot of* (with singular) (*?not much horse, ?quite a lot of horse*). So-called 'mass nouns', on the other hand, are normal with expressions of quantity but odd with expressions of numerousness (*not much milk, quite a lot of milk, ?two hundred milks, ?several milks*). One way of testing for the distinction is to ask whether some portion of X still counts as X. For instance, a portion of a litre of milk is still milk, but half a car is not a car. A 'count' interpretation involves thinking of something as coming in separate, bounded 'chunks' that can be counted; a 'mass' interpretation conceptualises something as a continuous 'substance' with no inherent boundaries. When we say *some chocolate*, we think of the chocolate as a continuous substance without inherent boundaries; when we say *two chocolates*, we think of the chocolates as distinct bounded entities. Most mass nouns in English are grammatically singular, but some are plural, such as *brains* (as in *It takes brains to do this job*), *guts, belongings, oats*. Although many nouns have a strong preference for either mass use or count use, many others can be used normally either way (*some wine* (mass), *some wines* (count)), or show only a weak preference.

counterfactual conditionals   These present the hypothetical consequences of a non-factual event or state of affairs: *If you had gone, you would have met her yourself; Had you gone, you would have met her yourself; If you lived in Manchester, you would be able to visit your mother every day.*

count nouns   see under **countability**

dative   see under **functional roles**

D

declarative   This is usually considered to be grammatically the most basic sentence form (*Pete is brave*, as opposed to *Is Pete brave?*, *Be brave, Pete!* or *How brave Pete is!*). Prototypically, the declarative form encodes a statement, that is, a **proposition**, together with a commitment to its truth. The basic meaning of a declarative is related to the meanings of explicit **performative verbs** such as *state*, *assert*, *declare*, *aver*, *announce*, and so on, but is more general than any of these. A declarative sentence can acquire extra illocutionary force through **implicature**, as in *There's ice on the road* uttered as a warning.

decoding idiom   see under **idiom**

de dicto **interpretation**   see under *de re* vs *de dicto* interpretations

deep cases   see **functional roles**

default meaning   The default meaning of a polysemous word is the meaning it is intuitively given in the absence of any context. For instance, the default meaning of the verb *see* is 'to have a visual experience (of)', although in particular contexts it can have other meanings, as in *I see what you mean, See what you can do, I think you should see a doctor*. The default meaning of a polysemous word is not necessarily the most frequently occurring meaning, but it is usually felt to be the most basic.

definite description   This is a sub-type of **definite referring expression**. The term usually denotes a noun phrase which refers to a definite entity (or group of entities), and which contains descriptive information necessary to identify the entity. The descriptive information may be carried by the head noun of the noun phrase, as in *that chimpanzee*, or it may be carried in part by adjectives or other modifiers, as in *that frail old man*.

definite reference   This is when one or more specific individual entities (persons, things, places, times, and so on) are referred to, as in the following (the definite referring expressions are in **bold**):

> I saw **Pete here yesterday**.
> **My husband** is in **London now**.
> Someone has stolen **the vase**.

The expressions *I*, *Pete*, *here*, *yesterday*, *my husband*, *London*, *now*, *the vase* all serve to refer to some individual entity whose identity forms an essential part of the message. To fully understand what is meant, the hearer must be able to pick out the correct 'referent' (that is, the entity referred to). A successful definite referring expression must contain enough information to allow the hearer to exclude all potential referents except the correct one. How much of this information needs to be given in the meaning of the expression depends on the context of utterance. In some contexts, the hearer needs very little help from linguistic meaning:

> A: Where's my pen?
> B: I haven't got it.

On other occasions, a lot more help is needed: *Could you pass me that book with the yellow cover at the far end of the top shelf?*

degree of membership   see under **prototype theory**

degrees of comparison   Traditionally, three degrees of comparison are recognised in connection with gradable adjectives and adverbs. These are 'positive' (*long*), 'comparative' (*longer*), and 'superlative' (*longest*). The comparative and superlative of longer adjectives and adverbs tend to be formed with *more* and *most* respectively (*more intelligent, most intelligent*). Superlatives can be divided into 'relative superlatives', as in *She is the cleverest of the three girls*, and 'absolute superlatives', where, strictly speaking, no comparison is involved, just a high degree of the property, as in *You have been most kind* or *His daughter is the sweetest little thing*. Comparatives and superlatives may be committed or impartial, according to whether the positive form would also apply. For instance, *longer* and *longest* are impartial because an item so described need not qualify for the description *long*. *Hotter* and *hottest*, on the other hand, are committed, since anything described as *hotter* or *hottest* has to be hot.

deixis, deictic expressions   Deictic expressions form a sub-type of **definite referring expressions**. They can be loosely thought of as expressions which 'point to' their referents. Usage of the term 'deixis' is variable, but most typically it designates referring expressions which indicate the location of referents along certain dimensions, using the speaker (and time and place of speaking) as a reference point or 'deictic centre' (this type of deixis is sometimes described as 'egocentric'). An example is the use of *this* and *that*. In *Can you pass me that newspaper*, the newspaper in question is typically relatively distant from the speaker; however, once the speaker receives the newspaper, any further reference to it will require a different deictic element: *I'm going to have to stop buying this newspaper*. A change of this sort, made necessary by a change in the relation between the referent and the speaker, is diagnostic for a deictic element (items like *this* and *that* are sometimes called 'shifters'). Some scholars treat the definite article *the* as a deictic element, although it does not strictly locate its referent along any particular dimension. Some scholars apply the term *deixis* to any expression which specifies a location, whether or not the specification is egocentric (e.g. *on the table, in the kitchen, in London*). Certain verbs of motion encode direction relative to one of the participants in a speech situation, and may thus be called deictic. For instance, *come* denotes motion towards either speaker or hearer (*Come and see me sometime, I'll come and see you tomorrow*), while *go* denotes motion towards a third person (*You/I should go and see him*). The verbs *bring* and *take* have a similar relation (*I'll bring it to you, I'll take it to him*). There are three main sub-types of deixis: **spatial**, **temporal**, and **person deixis**, and two minor sub-types: **social** and **discourse deixis**. Occasionally, the deictic centre is not the speaker (see under **projected deixis**).

denotation   The denotation of a linguistic expression is that aspect of its meaning which is involved in its potential for use in making true statements about the world. A distinction is made between two aspects of denotation. Take the word *dog*. This word can be used to refer to certain things but not others. The set of things the word properly applies to is known as its 'extension', in this case, the set of all dogs (the term 'denotation' is sometimes restricted to this). However, the word also denotes the property or properties something has to have in order to count as a dog (we can think of this as the **concept** DOG); this is called the 'intension' of the word (also sometimes called **connotation**). (The extension of a word is sometimes called its 'reference' and the intension its 'sense' – beware of the different uses of these terms.)

deontic modality   see under **modality**

de re vs *de dicto* **interpretations**   An utterance like *The prize cheque will be presented to the winner by the president of the company* has two interpretations corresponding to two readings of the phrase *the president of the company*. The first interpretation is that the phrase refers to the person who is president of the company at the time of the utterance, who may or may not still be president at the time of the presentation. This reading, which incorporates the current reference of the term, is known as a *de re* interpretation. The second interpretation is that whoever is president at the time of the presentation ceremony will present the cheque. This reading, which is committed only to the **intension** of the utterance, but leaves the **extension** open, is known as a *de dicto* reading.

derivation, derivational affix   see under **affix**

diachronic semantics   The study of the way the meanings of semantic expressions change over time. See **semantic change**.

diagnostic vs typical features   The diagnostic features of a category are those which distinguish it from all or most of its fellows; the typical features are those which all or most of the members of a category possess. Consider the category of birds. All birds lay eggs, so this is a typical feature. But so do many other creatures, so this feature does not single out the category of birds. On the other hand, only birds have feathers, so the possession of feathers is diagnostic for the category of birds (this feature is also typical). Both diagnosticity and typicality vary in degree. The possession of feathers is both maximally diagnostic and maximally typical. But having two legs, while diagnostic to some degree since most creatures have more than two legs, is not maximally diagnostic because it is shared with, for instance, humans.

dictionary meaning vs encyclopaedic meaning   This distinction usually applies to the meanings of words. As the names imply, the two sorts of meaning relate to what one might expect to find in a dictionary definition and an encyclopaedia entry respectively. Basically, encyclopaedic meaning is very broad, and in principle includes everything that is known about the referent of a word. This will obviously vary from speaker to speaker, but there may be a common core that all or most speakers from a particular community might be expected to share. The encyclopaedic meaning of, say, *dog* might include such matters as typical appearance and behaviour, how they should be looked after, the usefulness of dogs, legal aspects of dog ownership, the history of the domestication of dogs, and so on. In principle, the dictionary meaning of *dog* should include whatever is necessary to distinguish dogs from all other possibilities. In linguistic theory, the notion of dictionary meaning usually appears under the guise of the (semantic) content of a 'lexical entry' in an 'ideal lexicon', the purpose of which is to account for the linguistic semantic properties of a word from the perspective of some particular theory. For many linguists, these are confined to logical properties such as entailments. Some linguists, while accepting that certain aspects of the meaning of a word are more central than others, dispute the idea that a clear distinction can be drawn between information needed to account for the linguistic behaviour of a word and general knowledge about the referent of a word.

dimensions of (lexical) meaning   The semantic properties of a word can be grouped under three main headings: descriptive meaning, expressive meaning, and evocative meaning. (All three types can be present at the same time.)

1. The descriptive meaning of a word is that part of its meaning which constrains what it can be used to refer to, and which determines the truth values of statements which contain it. Descriptive meaning therefore includes **propositional meaning**, but it can be extended to include characteristic or proto-typical features, such as the barking of dogs, rather than simply logically necessary features, such as the fact that a dog is an animal. The most important dimensions of descriptive meaning are quality, specificity, intensity and vagueness:

   (a) Quality: what distinguishes, for instance, *red* from *yellow*, *dog* from *cat*, *plum* from *banana*, run from *walk*, *happy* from *disappointed*.

   (b) Specificity: what distinguishes **hyponyms** like *dog* and *daffodil* from their respective hyperonyms (superordinates) *animal* and *flower*; likewise, meronym-holonym pairs like *finger:hand* differ on this dimension.

   (c) Intensity: a special form of specificity. It is what distinguishes pairs like *fear: terror*, *dislike: hate*, *break: smash*.

   (d) Vagueness: appropriateness for approximate use. Consider the following: *Twenty-four people turned up for the meeting*; *A couple of dozen people turned up for the meeting*. A dictionary is likely to define *a dozen* as 'twelve'. But suppose twenty-three or twenty-five people turned up: the first sentence would be false, but the second would be true (there is a similar difference between *a couple of* and *two*).

2. Expressive meaning is exemplified by exclamations like *Wow!*, *Shit!*, *Ouch!*, and so on; by expletives used as modifiers, as in *It's bloody cold in here*; and by expressions such as *to stuff oneself*, as in *He just sat there stuffing himself and not saying a word* (compare *eat a hearty meal*). Expressive meaning expresses some emotion, judgement, or attitude, but in a non-propositional way. That is to say it does not contribute to the **propositional meaning** of the utterance, and therefore does not affect its truth value. Expressive meaning is valid only for the speaker at the moment of utterance. For instance, *What the hell are you doing here?* expresses negative surprise on the part of the speaker. But even if the question is directed at a past event, as in *What the hell was he doing there?*, the surprise expressed is valid only for the moment of speaking (i.e. expressive meaning does not exhibit **displacement**).

3. Evocative meaning denotes words specific to, or specially characteristic of, particular language varieties such as dialects and registers that have the power to evoke their usual contexts (think of the difference between *dale* and *glen*, or *kick the bucket* and *pass away*).

diminutive affix   An affix which modifies the meaning of a noun to make it refer to a smaller or less important version of what the unaffixed noun denotes. In English the main diminutive suffixes are: *-ling* (*duck: duckling*), *-ette* (*kitchen: kitchenette*), *-let* (*tart: tartlet*), *-ie* (*lad: laddie*). *Mini-* is a diminutive prefix (*skirt: miniskirt*).

Diminutives are often used to express affection or intimacy, rather than (or as well as) small size (*dog: doggy*, *puss: pussy*, *pig: piggy*), and are especially characteristic of talk with children. The term 'diminutive' is often applied to a word bearing a diminutive affix. It also applies to 'short forms' of proper names (*James: Jim*, *Margaret: Peggy*).

directional opposites   The main types of directional opposite are opposite directions, antipodals, and reversives.

1. Opposite directions are adverbial pairs such as *up: down, forwards: backwards, north: south, in: out, clockwise: anticlockwise, left: right*, which denote potential orientations or paths of movement in contrary directions.

2. Antipodals represent extreme points along a certain axis within some entity. Purely spatial examples include *top: bottom, front: back, floor: ceiling, nose: tail, head: toe*, but the relationship can also be seen in non-spatial domains: *beginning: end* (e.g. of a novel or a concert), *introduction: conclusion, black: white* (on a continuous scale with shades of grey between the extremes).

3. Reversives involve movement or change (or cause of movement or change) in opposite directions between two states. Like antipodals they may involve literal motion, as in *rise: fall* (e.g. in water level), *advance: retreat, ascend: descend, arrive: depart, enter: leave, embark: disembark, mount: dismount*, or they may involve non-spatial change, as in *lighten: darken, heat (up): cool (down), improve: deteriorate*. For a reversive relation it is not necessary for the path of change to be the same for both items as long as the initial and final states

are reversed. For instance, the action of *untying* a knot is not normally the exact reversal of the action of *tying* it.

Some lexical **converses** (e.g. *buy: sell*) have a directional component.

disambiguation   see under **ambiguity**

discourse deixis   This is when reference is made to discourse items which occur either before or after the current time of speaking. When functioning as discourse deictics, *that* typically refers to a previously occurring item, and *this* to something which is still to come: *That was the best story I've heard for a long time, Wait till you hear this ...* Expressions such as *therefore, however, on the other hand*, which relate portions of earlier discourse to portions of later discourse, are sometimes included under discourse deictics.

discourse markers   A category of expressions which includes such items as *well, oh, then, so, but*. They are grammatically optional, in that omitting them does not result in ungrammaticality, and they mark boundaries between units of discourse. Among their typical functions are:

1. They carry expressive meaning (they may also have **propositional meaning**).
2. They contribute to, or emphasise **coherence** relations in discourse.
3. They act as **constraints on relevance**.
   (These are not mutually exclusive.)

discrete vs continuous signs   Continuous signs can vary in a gradual way along at least one dimension, and each perceptible change entails a meaning change. Take the case of a smile. This can vary in 'breadth' from the merest hint of a smile to a broad grin, and all the intermediate stages indicate a particular degree of amusement (or whatever). The same is true of how loudly we shout when we say *Ouch!* Discrete signs can only vary in separate jumps, and intermediate forms (if they exist) do not have intermediate meaning. Most linguistic signs (all words) are discrete in this sense. One can move in a way that gradually changes from a walk into a run, but one cannot gradually change the word *walk* into the word *run* (and even if we could, the resulting intermediate stages would not designate something between a run and a walk).

displacement   This is one of the key features distinguishing human language from, for instance, animal communication. It is the ability to speak about things that are not present (*There are no horses here*) and about times and places other than the 'here and now' (*I met her last summer in New York*), as well as about hypothetical entities and events. (Not all aspects of meaning can be 'displaced' – see under **dimensions of (lexical) meaning**.)

distributive plural   see under **plural**

domain (cognitive)   Any coherent body of conceptual content which serves as an essential background for, or is presupposed by, some individual concept or conceptual process. For specific examples, see under **frame semantics, profile and base, Conceptual Metaphor Theory**.

dot-objects   These are associated particularly with the work of Pustejovsky. They are related to global senses with **facets**, but are viewed from a different perspective. They are entities like *book* that belong simultaneously to more than one distinct taxonomy (in this case, the taxonomy of texts and the taxonomy of physical objects) without being ambiguous in the normal sense. This duality is specified in a 'generative lexicon' under the **formal role**, and is conventionally indicated thus: [PHYSICAL OBJECT•TEXT] (hence the name 'dot-object'). Each of these aspects of meaning has a different specification under the remaining **qualia roles**. For instance, under the **constitutive role**, the parts of a text are different from the parts of a physical book; under the **telic role**, the function of a text is to be read, but the function of the physical book is to give the text a physical form; under the **agentive role**, a book as text originates in a process of writing, but the physical book originates in a process of printing, binding, and so on.

dual   *Dual* is a term in the **number system** of some languages which indicates exactly two of whatever is being counted. One language with a dual is Classical Arabic: *rajulun* ('a man'), *rajuleen* ('two men'). All languages that have a dual also have at least a **singular** and a **plural**.

durative   A durative verb denotes an action or process or state that is thought of as continuing over a period of time, rather than instantaneously: *Pete lay motionless*, *Liz lives in Manchester*, *Pete resembles his father*, *Liz knows the answer*, *It's raining*.

dysphemism   A term or expression that expresses negative feelings or attitude towards the referent, such as *bitch* for 'woman', or *rag* for 'newspaper'.

E

eavesdropper   see under **speech event participant**

egocentricity (of deixis)   see under **deixis**

ellipsis   This depends on a conventional notion of a 'complete sentence'. Ellipsis occurs when an utterance takes the form of an incomplete sentence, usually in a situation where (a) the missing parts are essential to the correct interpretation of the utterance and (b) the hearer can easily recover them. Answers to questions are often elliptical:

> A: How do you feel now?
> B: Awful.

The 'full' form of B's answer is *I feel awful*. Cases where an essential piece of information must be recovered by the hearer are not considered elliptical if it is not usual to provide this information explicitly. For instance, *Isn't Pete tall!* requires a reference point for *tall* – tall relative to what? The answer could depend, for instance, on how old Pete is. But this information is not normally encoded, so *Isn't Pete tall!* is not considered elliptical.

emergent meaning   see under **blending (conceptual)**

encoding idiom   see under **idiom**

encyclopaedic knowledge   see under **dictionary meaning vs encyclopaedic meaning**

entailment   A logical relation between **propositions**. A proposition P entails a proposition Q, if and only if the truth of Q follows inescapably from the truth of P. For instance, if P is 'Pete killed the wasp' and Q is 'The wasp died', then if P is true, Q must also be true, and if Q is false, P must also be false. Notice, however, that strictly speaking there is no logical relation between the sentences *Pete killed the wasp* and *The wasp died*, although one often encounters statements to that effect. The logical relationship holds between the propositions expressed by these sentences only if they are about the same wasp on the same occasion. For a proposition P to entail a proposition Q it is not enough for the truth of Q to be merely an expected consequence. For instance, 'X is a bird' does not entail 'X can fly', even though most birds can fly. (Compare **material implication**.)

entrenchment (also called **establishment**)   This refers to the degree to which something (form or meaning) is permanently recorded in some sort of mental store. The process of laying down is presumed to be a gradual one and depends on frequency of usage – the more often a new form or meaning is used, the more entrenched it becomes. A new coinage or a new use of an existing form cannot be produced by looking it up in a store – it must be created by some constructive process. Once entrenched, it can be retrieved from the store as required, and this is presumed to be easier and faster than creating it from scratch. Compare the bold item in *I find him a bit old womanish* to the similar item in *I find him rather retired colonelish*. Both are (presumably) understandable, but the former is more entrenched and is comprehended with greater ease.

epistemic modality   see under **modality**

equipollent antonyms   A sub-type of **antonym (2)**. As in the case of **overlapping antonyms**, each term operates on its own scale, but unlike the overlapping type the scales point outwards from a common zero value rather than overlap. For instance, there is a scale of hotness and a scale of coldness pointing in the opposite direction, the zero value of both scales corresponding to the absence of a temperature sensation. Typical examples are *hot: cold*; *sweet: sour*; *happy: sad*. Of all types of antonym, the equipollent type shows the greatest degree of symmetry between the two terms, hence most symptoms of **polarity** are absent. For instance, both terms are committed in the comparative (for something to be *hotter* than something else, it must be *hot*, and likewise with *colder* and *cold*) and both yield committed *how*-questions: *How hot is it?* and *How cold is it?* presume hotness and coldness respectively. Equipollent antonyms are the least frequent type in English (some languages, such as Turkish, do not appear to have any); most of them refer to sensations or emotions.

equipollent opposition   see under **markedness**

essentialism (psychological)   This is a theory about the nature of concepts (see also under the **'theory' theory**). It proposes that human beings, in their use of concepts, act on the assumption that for every conceptual category there is an essence which is shared by every member of the category. Hence, there is an essence of 'salt-hood', an essence of 'hammer-hood', an essence of 'giraffe-hood', and so on. For many categories, the essence is 'hidden', in two senses: (1) it may not be directly observable; (2) it may not be known to the user. In either case, the user has faith in its existence and, presumably, in its knowability (by appropriate experts). The nature of an essence depends on the ontological domain of the concept, that is, what kind of thing it is. For instance, the essence of giraffe-hood is passed down from parents to offspring – something with giraffe parents is a giraffe, whatever it looks like; we would also expect giraffe offspring to have giraffe innards. Most educated people would expect the essence of giraffe-hood to have something to do with DNA, but savannah-dwellers with no knowledge of modern genetics have the same belief in an essence. The essence of an artefact like a hammer is tied up with its intended function. Asked to imagine a giraffe whose neck and legs are shortened, and which is treated so that it develops black and white stripes on its back, people are resistant to the notion that the animal has changed into a zebra. On the other hand, they are willing to accept that a hammer whose metal head is filed down to the form of a chisel has in fact been turned into a chisel.

establishment   see **entrenchment**

etymology   The study of the historical origins of words and changes in their meaning and use after their introduction into a language. It includes what in modern linguistics is called **semantic change,** or **diachronic semantics**, but is particularly associated with more traditional approaches. The word can also apply to the history of a particular word.

euphemism   An expression that refers to something that people hesitate to mention lest it cause offence, but which lessens the offensiveness by referring indirectly in some way. The most common topics for which we use euphemisms are sexual activity and sex organs, and bodily functions such as defecation and urination, but euphemisms can also be found in reference to death, aspects of religion and money. The main strategies of indirectness are **metonymy**, **generalisation**, **metaphor** and phonological deformation.

Sex:
intercourse	*go to bed with* (metonymy), *do it* (generalisation)
penis	*His member was clearly visible* (generalisation)

Bodily function:
defecate	*go to the toilet* (metonymy), *use the toilet* (generalisation)

Death:
die	*pass away* (metaphor), *He's no longer with us* (generalisation)

Religion:
God	*gosh, golly* (phonological deformation)
Jesus	*gee whiz* (phonological deformation)
Hell	*heck* (phonological deformation)

event-types   In the description of verb aspect a number of event-types are distinguished, according to the way the event unfolds through time. Here five event-types will be described: states, activities, accomplishments, achievements, and semelfactives. Three event-types are construed as **durative**, that is, as happening over a period of time rather than being instantaneous: states, activities and accomplishments.

1. States: these represent the limiting case of an event, since nothing 'happens'. A state has no inherent beginning or end, and no change occurs, as in *Pete lives in London*.
2. Activities: these have no inherent beginning or end (such events are also called 'atelic'), but unlike in a state, things 'happen': *Pete teaches French*.
3. Accomplishments: like activities, these involve

something happening, but unlike activities, are construed as having a definite point of completion (such events are also called 'telic'). If V represents an accomplishment, then to V in (time interval) is typically more normal than to X for (time interval): *Pete wrote the letter in half an hour*, *?Pete wrote the letter for half an hour*. With activities, the normalities are reversed: *Liz practised the piano for an hour*, *?Liz practised the piano in an hour*. Another diagnostic feature of accomplishments is their behaviour with *stop* and *finish*. Both verbs yield normal sentences (*Pete finished washing the dishes*, *Pete stopped washing the dishes*), but the latter implies that the job was not completed. Activities are typically odd with *finish* (*Liz ?finished laughing*, *Liz stopped laughing*) unless some definite period of time can be plausibly construed (*Liz has finished practising the piano* (she does two hours every day)).

The remaining two event-types are construed as **punctual**, that is, as happening instantaneously:

4. Achievements: these involve a change from one state to another: *The guests departed*, *The building collapsed*, *The wounded soldier died*.
5. Semelfactives: these denote an instantaneous event that does not involve a change of state: *Pete blinked/sneezed/coughed*, *Liz clapped her hands*.

exclamations   Grammatical exclamations in English are introduced either by *How.....!* or *What ....!*, together with a special word order:

How tall he is!
How he dominates the stage!

What an actor he is!
What a wonderful time we had!
What dreadful weather!

The semantic function of an exclamation is to express an extreme emotion or attitude to some presupposed fact, very often with a component of surprise, combined with either strong approval or disapproval.

exclusive first person plurals   see under **person deixis**

exemplar theory   This is a theory about the nature and structure of **concepts**, one of several proposals aimed at remedying the shortcomings of the **classical theory** of concepts (see also **prototype theory**, the 'theory' theory). The basic idea is that a concept is represented not as a set of features (as in prototype theory) but as a collection of memory traces of individual examples. The centrality of an item, on this approach, is given by its overall similarity to the set of stored examples, and the prototype is the example with the greatest similarity to the largest number of other examples. Overall resemblance to a range of examples yields the same prediction of **verification speed** and degree of **priming** as does the number of prototype features possessed. Generally speaking, exemplar theory is as successful as prototype theory in explaining **prototype effects**, since both appeal to similarity as the main factor. It is therefore difficult to devise experiments to discriminate between them. However, exemplar theory does give a better account in certain circumstances. For instance, if two salient features of a category are both fairly frequent, both will appear in the prototype representation. But suppose they never or rarely co-occur. Prototype theory would predict that an example having both features would be recognised quickly even though it was atypical; exemplar theory would predict a slower categorisation because of the lack of examples having both features.

exophora   see under **anaphora**

experiencer   see under **functional roles**

explicature   see under **relevance theory**

extension   see under **denotation**

F

facets   These are aspects of the meaning of a word belonging to different **ontological types** that sometimes behave in an independent way and thus give an appearance of ambiguity, while at other times seem to be fused into a single global concept. An example of this is provided by the word *book*, which has a 'physical object' meaning, as in *Pete picked up the book*, and an 'abstract text' meaning, as in *Pete found the book amusing*. Both of these are central to the everyday concept BOOK, and they are simultaneously present in *Pete was sitting in the lounge reading a book*. But they can behave independently, as in *a new book*, which is ambiguous between a newly produced physical book in pristine condition and a newly published text (irrespective of its physical condition). Facets typically have different sense relations. For instance, *novel* is a **hyponym** of the 'abstract text' facet of *book*, while *paperback* is a hyponym of the 'physical object' facet. (Words with facets are also known as **dot-objects**.)

factitive   see under **functional roles**

family resemblance   see under **prototype theory**

felicity conditions   These are conditions that must be satisfied for a **speech act** to be properly performed (also
known as 'happiness conditions'). They can be grouped
under three headings: preparatory conditions, sincerity
conditions, and essential conditions.

1. Preparatory conditions define an appropriate
   setting for the act, including the speaker's in-
   tentions and qualifications. For instance, someone
   uttering the words *I pronounce you man and wife*
   has not sealed the union of a man and a woman
   unless he or she is properly qualified, and does so in
   the course of an official marriage ceremony; the
   issuer of a command must have authority over the
   addressee, and the act must be both possible and
   not already carried out. If the preparatory conditions are not satisfied, the speech act has not been
   validly performed (it is said to have 'misfired').
2. Sincerity conditions require the speaker to be
   sincere: someone who promises to do something
   must genuinely intend to do it; someone congratulating someone must feel pleasure at that person's
   good luck or success; someone making a statement
   must believe it to be true, and so on. An insincere
   speech act has nonetheless been performed, but the
   speaker is guilty of an 'abuse'.
3. Essential conditions define the essential nature of
   the speech act. For instance, if someone makes a
   promise, they must intend their utterance to count
   as putting them under an obligation to carry out
   what is promised; in the case of *I name this ship ...*
   the speaker must intend the utterance to count as
   conferring a name on the ship; in making a state-

ment, a speaker must intend it to be taken as true, and so on. If the essential conditions for a particular speech act are not met, then merely producing the right form of utterance does not result in the speech act being performed. For instance, producing *The King of France is bald* in a logic class would not normally count as a statement committing the speaker to its truth. Notice that this is different from sincerity: someone telling a lie intends their statement to be taken as the truth.

fictive motion   This is when something is described as moving or changing in some way, although it is, in reality, perfectly static: the only 'movement' is either in the perception of the speaker, or is purely imaginary. Take the case of *The road goes over the hill*. Of course the road does not move, but the speaker visualises a journey along it. A slightly different case is illustrated by *At this point the road narrows*. Again, there is no actual change in the width of the road at any given point, but a traveller along the road will experience a narrowing of the representation of the road in his visual field. The phenomenon is not confined to motion as such. Any sort of change may be involved: *The condition of the road surface deteriorates as you approach the crossroads.*

figurative language, figure of speech   Linguistic expressions are said to be figurative, or used figuratively, if their intended meaning is (a) something other than their **literal meaning** and (b) can be understood on the basis of generally applicable principles of meaning extension (rather than an ad hoc arrangement, for instance between Pete and Liz before a party so that if Liz says *I love that picture* she means 'I want to go home now'). Many figures of speech are recognised in the study of rhetoric, but the main ones that have attracted the attention of linguists are: **euphemism, hyperbole, irony, metaphor, metonymy, simile,** and **understatement**.

figure and ground   These notions were introduced by the gestalt psychologists in their account of perception. The basic idea is that any act of perception involves the highlighting of some portion of the perceptual field (the figure) and the backgrounding of the rest (the ground). Attention is focused on the figure, which is thereby more fully present to consciousness than the ground. The cognitive linguistic notions of **profile** and **base**, and **trajector** and **landmark** are developments of this basic notion. (Some linguists draw a distinction between figure (vs ground), focus of attention, and foreground (vs background), but the arguments are too subtle and complex to go into here.)

flouting the (conversational) maxims   Some **conversational implicatures** arise when a speaker tries as far as possible to follow the **maxims of conversation**, but others can arise when a speaker deliberately goes against one or more of the maxims, provided that (1) it is clear to the hearer that the 'flouting' is deliberate and (2) the speaker can nonetheless be assumed to be obeying the **Co-operative Principle** and is therefore breaking the rules for good communicative reasons. Consider the following:

A: Where did you go last night?
B: Out.

In some circumstances B's reply could be taken as a signal of non-co-operation, equivalent to *Mind your own business*. But a situation can easily be imagined where B gives no sign of opting out of the conversation. Suppose Grandma, who has firm ideas about how teenage girls like B should and should not spend their evenings, is within earshot. B's reply could then be interpreted as 'I'd rather not say while Grandma is listening.' In many cases, deliberate flouting of one or more maxims is a signal that an utterance is not to be interpreted literally. For instance, if interpreted literally, *Boys will be boys* gives no information at all, *That man is a snake* and *The chicken salad in the corner wants his coffee now* are obviously untrue, and *Oh, brilliant!* is not a relevant comment when someone's 'repair' of the toaster has resulted in the lights fusing. But all make sense with appropriate non-literal readings.

focal region   Applied to a category, this indicates the grouping of central or prototypical examples.

focus   see under **foregrounding**

force   see under **functional roles**

force dynamics   This is a way of looking at events in terms of the forces (physical or metaphorical) acting on or between participants. The following illustrate some of the basic force relations:

> Liz picked up the cup. (Liz applied force to the cup.)
> Liz held the cup. (Liz acted to prevent some presumed external force from affecting the cup.)
> Liz dropped the cup. (Liz allowed an external force to move the cup.)
> The cup fell. (The speaker construes the event as happening spontaneously.)

These notions can be extended to non-physical events:

> The government has raised the price of oil.

The government has acted to maintain the price of oil.
The government has allowed the price of oil to fall.
The price of oil has fallen.

foregrounding (sometimes called 'highlighting')   There are various linguistic devices for increasing the **salience** of part of an utterance. One obvious device is to pronounce it with emphatic stress:

PETE did the washing up yesterday.
Pete did THE WASHING UP yesterday.
Pete did the washing up YESTERDAY.

(Notice that these different forms not only highlight different items, but also introduce different **presuppositions**. Foregrounding can also be achieved grammatically:

It was Pete who did the washing up yesterday.
It was yesterday that Pete did the washing up.
What Pete did yesterday was the washing up.
It was the washing up that Pete did yesterday.

Structures like those illustrated above are called 'focusing devices', and the foregrounded part of the utterance is called the 'focus'.

formal role   see under **qualia roles**

formal semantics   This is an approach to semantics which aims to model natural language meanings and their properties by means of a system (or systems) of logic. See under **propositional calculus, predicate calculus, Montague semantics**.

frame semantics   This is a theory of meaning which holds that word meanings can only be properly understood and described against the background of a particular body of knowledge and assumptions (known as a 'frame'). For instance, it might seem at first sight that 'unmarried man' is an obvious definition of *bachelor*. But on closer examination this definition raises some awkward questions. Is the Pope a bachelor? Would we apply the term to an unmarried man known to be gay (assuming that gay marriages are not yet accepted)? Or even to an eighteen-year-old unmarried male student? Probably not – yet they are all unmarried men. However, the definition makes more sense if it is set against a background of social customs that characterise certain men as 'marriageable'; *bachelor* can then be defined as 'an unmarried marriageable man'. Because this frame presents a selective picture that does not encompass all the possible social statuses of adult males, it is sometimes described as an 'idealised cognitive model (ICM)'. As another instance of the frame-dependence of meaning, consider the case of *dead* and *alive*. We might feel confident in assuming that if something is not alive, then it is dead. However, a chair is not alive, yet we would not normally describe it as 'dead'. Here, the appropriate frame is the domain of living things: if something animate is not alive then it is dead. According to frame semantics all word meanings have this character.

free variable   see under **variable**

frozen metaphors   see under **idioms**

function (semantic, logical)   This is used in two main ways: (1) equivalent to **predicate** or (2) a logical formula consisting of constants and **variables** which yields a **proposition** when values are assigned to the variables (see under **predicate logic**).

functional roles These are also called 'case roles', 'deep cases', 'participant roles', or 'thematic roles'. They represent ways in which the nouns closely related to a verb (for instance, its subject, object(s), and complement, but excluding **circumstantial roles**) are semantically related to the meaning of the verb. An examination of a wide range of the world's languages suggests that there is a limited number of possible functional roles. Typically, a particular functional role can be represented only once in a sentence, and a particular noun can only fulfil one role. The number of roles and their labels differ from linguist to linguist, but the following are representative:

AGENT, AGENTIVE: the participant in an event who is seen as the (typically) animate 'doer' of the action, such as *Pete* in *Pete stroked the cat*.

INSTRUMENT/INSTRUMENTAL: something inanimate used by an agent in carrying out an action, such as *knife* in *Pete cut a hole in the box with a knife* and *key* in *This key will open the door*.

FORCE: an inanimate doer, such as *the wind* in *The wind blew the door shut*. (FORCE was originally included under INSTRUMENT.)

EXPERIENCER: an animate participant in an event affected in a characteristically animate way, such as *Pete* in *Pete saw the crocodile*, *The story amused Pete*, *Pete was terrified by the storm*.

BENEFICIARY: an animate participant for whose sake an action is performed, such as *us* in *Pete cooked us a splendid meal*. (BENEFICIARY and EXPERIENCER are sometimes included under DATIVE.)

LOCATION, LOCATIVE: the place most relevant to an event, such as *London* in *Pete lives in London*. Three subdivisions are often recognised: (1) SOURCE (the starting point or origin of an event), such as *Pete* in *Pete left London several years ago*, or *the computer* in *The computer gives out a lot of heat*; (2) PATH, such as *Liz* in *Liz climbed the wall*; and (3) GOAL, such as *the hotel* in *We didn't reach the hotel until nearly midnight* or *the table* in *Place the gun on the table*.

PATIENT: the inanimate participant affected by an event, but which does not undergo a change of state, such as *the letter* in *Jane hastily hid the letter when she heard the knock at the door*.

THEME: the inanimate participant affected by an event and which undergoes a change of state, such as *the window panes* in *The blast shattered the window panes*. This includes what was originally called FACTITIVE, where something comes into being as a result of the event, such as *a splendid meal* in *Pete cooked us a splendid meal*. (PATIENT and THEME were originally included under OBJECTIVE.)

fuzzy boundaries The boundaries of many everyday **conceptual categories** are not well-defined (for example, between what ages is someone correctly described as *middle-aged*?). This characteristic goes along with a lack of clear diagnostic criteria for membership (Wittgenstein's famous example of this was GAME). Typical symptoms of fuzziness are: subjective uncertainty on the part of speakers about whether certain items belong to the category or not; disagreement between speakers regarding membership; and different judgements by a given speaker on different occasions and in different contexts. The fuzziness of category boundaries is cited by the proponents of **prototype theory** as evidence against the **classical theory** of category structure.

G

gender   Grammatical gender is a property of nouns in some languages. The gender of a noun mainly affects grammatical agreement, between a noun and accompanying adjectives and articles, for instance, and pronominal reference (that is, reference by means of a pronoun). In French, the form of the adjective and the article in the following vary according to the gender of the noun:

> la maison blanche ('the white house') (feminine noun)
> le batiment blanc ('the white building') (masculine noun)

Likewise, the form of the italicised pronoun in the following depends on the gender of the antecedent noun:

> J'ai acheté ce vieux livre [masculine noun] hier. *Il* était vraiment bon marché.
> 'I bought this old book yesterday. It was really cheap.'
> J'ai acheté cette table [feminine noun] hier. *Elle* était vraiment bon marché.
> 'I bought this table yesterday. It was really cheap.'

A variety of gender systems are found in the world's languages, but the majority are correlated with sex or **animacy**. A distinction is commonly drawn between 'grammatical gender' and 'natural gender'. The former is determined solely by grammatical behaviour, the latter by features of the referent. There is usually some correlation between these two, but only a partial one. For instance, in French there is no obvious 'natural' reason for *livre* to be masculine and *table* feminine; the classic case in German is *Löffel*, meaning 'spoon' (masculine), *Gabel*, 'fork' (feminine), and *Messer*, 'knife' (neuter). On the other hand there is a strong tendency in both languages for nouns referring to female persons such as

mother, sister, and so on to be feminine and nouns referring to male persons to be masculine. In English, gender
only appears in pronominal reference, but the fact that
pronoun use is predictable from meaning leads some to
say that English does not have gender and others to say
that it has natural gender.

generalisation   see under **semantic change**

generalised vs particularised conversational implicatures   A
distinction can be drawn between two types of **conversational implicature**. An implicature counts as 'generalised' if it is a default reading, that is to say it arises
unless it is explicitly cancelled and is to that extent independent of context. For instance, *Some of the parents
came to the meeting* will normally imply that not all of
them did. But in *Some of the parents, if not all of them,
came to the meeting* the implicature 'not all' is cancelled.
The fact that this is not anomalous shows that we are not
dealing with an **entailment**. A 'particularised' implicature is one that depends on specific contexts and is not a
default message component. For instance, *Jane is in the
shower* does not convey a default message component
'She cannot come to the telephone'. This requires a
particular context:

A: Can I speak to Jane?
B: She's in the shower.

Generalised conversational implicatures can be further
divided into I-implicatures, M-implicatures, and Q-
implicatures. (These labels relate to Grice's maxims
of conversation. I-implicatures are concerned with infor-
mativeness (see the Maxim of Quality); M-implicatures
relate to Grice's Maxim of Manner; Q-implicatures
relate to his Maxim of Quantity.)

1. I-implicatures depend on the notion that we do not need to spell out what the hearer would expect to be normally the case. For instance, in the case of *This car costs £15,000*, we do not need to be told that the price includes the wheels, or that the chicken in *The chicken we had at the weekend was delicious* was (a) dead and (b) cooked.

2. M-implicatures are based on the principle that if a speaker avoids a standard way of saying something, then they do not wish to convey the standard meaning. For instance, if an offering at breakfast is described as 'partially charred pieces of bread', rather than 'toast' we are entitled to assume that it somehow falls short of standard expectations for toast.

3. Q-implicatures depend on the principle that a speaker will make the strongest possible statement that is consistent with the facts. For instance, *Pete has three children* normally implies 'Pete has no more than three children'. However, in special circumstances, this implicature may be suppressed, as in

   A: You have to have three children to qualify for this allowance.
   B: Pete has three children.

B's reply is perfectly justified if Pete has five children. (Notice that the '*some* implicates *not all*' example cited above falls under this heading.) Q-implicatures like these, which depend on a scale of values of some sort, are known as 'scalar implicatures'. The so-called 'clausal implicatures' also fall under this heading. For instance, 'If P then Q' implicates that the stronger statement 'P, therefore Q' cannot validly be made. *If Pete left early, he won't have got the message* implicates that the stronger statement *Pete left early, so he won't have got the message* cannot be made.

generative grammar   The aim of a generative grammar is to provide a structural description of each of the infinite set of grammatical expressions of a language by means of a finite lexicon which lists the basic elements and their properties, and a finite set of rules for combining these elements. A complete generative grammar also provides a specification of the meaning of each expression. All word meanings are specified in terms of **semantic components** of one kind or another. The possible ways of combining these are indicated by **selectional restrictions**. For a modern version of a semantically explicit generative grammar see Jackendoff's **conceptual semantics**. For some recent refinements to the lexicon associated with a generative grammar, see **qualia roles** and **dot-objects**.

generic reference   This is where reference is made to a whole class of referents, rather than to a specific (or non-specific) individual or group of individuals, as is the case with **definite** and **indefinite reference**. The main ways of signalling generic reference in English are as follows:

1. Llamas are native to South America.
2. The llama is native to South America.
3. A frightened llama will attack its owner.

There are two ways of talking about a class of entities. We can say things that are true of every individual member of the class (or most of them), or we can say things that are only true of the class as a whole. Any of the above modes of generic reference can be used for the first of these:

Tigers have long tails.
The tiger has a long tail.
A tiger has a long tail.

But only the first two are normal with properties that hold only for the whole class:

Dodos are extinct.
The dodo is extinct.
*A dodo is extinct.

Generosity Maxim   see under **Tact and Generosity Maxims**

gestural deixis   This refers to the use of a **deictic** expression in a situation where, prototypically, speaker and hearer are together and the hearer can see what the speaker is doing. Gestural deixis, as the name implies, typically involves a gesture on the part of the speaker. Examples are: *It was this big* (speaker indicates a size with his hands); *I want you, you, and you to come with me* (speaker points to three people); *This is totally unacceptable* (speaker points to an offensive poster). An example involving **temporal deixis** which does not strictly demand co-presence of speaker and hearer (it could be done by telephone) but does require moment-by-moment monitoring of the situation by the hearer is: *Press the button ... (pause) ... NOW!* See also **symbolic deixis**.

given vs new information   These notions are concerned with what is called the 'information structure' of utterances. In virtually all utterances, some items are assumed by the speaker to be already present in the consciousness of the hearer, mostly as a result of previous discourse, and these constitute a platform for the presentation of new information. As the discourse proceeds, the new information of one utterance can become the given information for subsequent utterances, and so on. The distinction between given and new information can be marked linguistically in various ways. The indefinite article typically marks new information, and the definite article, given information: *A man and a woman entered the room. The man was smoking a pipe.* A pronoun used **anaphorically** indicates given information: *A man entered the room. He looked around for a vacant seat.* The stress pattern of an utterance can indicate new and given information (in the following example capitals indicate stress):

PETE washed the dishes. (in answer to *Who washed the dishes?*)

Pete washed the DISHES. (in answer to *What did Pete do?*)

Givenness is a matter of degree. Sometimes the degree of givenness is so great that the given item(s) can be omitted altogether (ellipsis):

A: What did you get for Christmas?
B: A computer. (The full form would be *I got a computer for Christmas.*)

goodness-of-exemplar (GOE) ratings To obtain GOE ratings, experimental subjects are asked to indicate how good something is as an example of a category, by giving it a numerical score on a 7-point scale. Number 1 on the scale indicates 'a very good example', 2, 'a good example', and so on down to 6, ' a poor example', and finally 7, 'a very poor example, not an example at all'. The scores are averaged over a large number of subjects. Provided the subjects have a similar cultural background and belong to a homogeneous speech community the scores for particular items cluster strongly around particular values, rather than being randomly distributed. This technique has been used to determine category prototypes. GOE score has been shown to correlate with other significant psychological properties (see **prototype effects**).

gradable adjectives   Gradable adjectives are adjectives that denote properties that can vary in degree or intensity, such as temperature, weight, speed, accuracy, safety, politeness, and so on (gradability is also a property of many adverbs). They typically can be inflected for **degrees of comparison** (*hot, hotter, hottest*), and can be modified (without oddness) by lexical **intensifiers** (*fairly hot, quite hot, rather hot, very hot, extremely hot*). Gradable adjectives are also normally **relative adjectives** because they cannot be understood except in conjunction with their head noun.

gradable contraries   see under **antonyms, antonymy (2)**

grammatical gender   see under **gender**

grammatical meaning   This is usually contrasted with **lexical meaning**. It does not, however, have a single, consistent usage. The main ways of using the expression are as follows:

1. The meanings carried by grammatical (or **closed set**) elements, such as affixes, prepositions, articles, conjunctions, and the like. These are typically very basic meanings which are compatible with a wide range of more specific lexical meanings.
2. The meanings words have by virtue of belonging to a particular grammatical category, especially noun,

verb, and adjective. On the one hand, it is clear that definitions of grammatical categories on the lines of 'a noun is a word that refers to a person, place, or thing; a verb refers to an action; an adjective refers to a property' do not work, either cross-linguistically or within a particular language. For instance, *punch* in *a punch* clearly refers to an action, but is a noun; *belong* is a verb, but does not refer to an action, and so on. There are two ways of defending this notion of grammatical meaning. One is to say that the prototypical noun refers to a person, place, or thing, a prototypical verb refers to an action, and a prototypical adjective to a quality. Another is to point to the palpable difference between, say, *a punch* and *to punch*. Although they both in some way refer to the same thing, in the former the action is construed as static, while in the latter the action is construed as dynamic. In other words, the categories indicate different ways of viewing referents, rather than aspects of the referents themselves.

3. The meanings of grammatical constructions, over and above the meanings of constituent lexical items. This may be very abstract information. For instance, an adjective-noun combination is generally to be interpreted as a modifier-head combination. However, proponents of Construction Grammar recognise constructions with much more specific meanings, such as *The X-er the Y-er*, as in *the bigger the better*.

4. The meaning conveyed by syntactic functions such as subject and object (of verb) or the **case** of nouns. This typically concerns **functional roles**, but the relation between syntactic functions and semantic functional roles is not straightforward. It is not the

case, for instance, that the subject of a verb in the **active voice** is always an **agent**:

> This key will open the door. (subject = INSTRU-MENT)
> Liz heard the gunshot. (subject = EXPERIENCER)
> Manchester lies further east than Edinburgh. (subject = LOCATION)
> The door opened. (subject = THEME)
> The glass broke. (subject = PATIENT)

However, there is a broad generalisation: the subject (of a verb in the active voice) is always the noun phrase with the 'most active' functional role in the sentence. Functional roles can be ordered in terms of their degree of activity: AGENT > INSTRU-MENT > EXPERIENCER, BENEFICIARY > LOCATION > PATIENT, THEME. This means that if there is an agent present, that will automatically become subject; if there is no agent but there is an instrument, then it will be subject, and so on down the line.

grammatical performativity   This refers to the signalling of illocutionary force by grammatical means. See under **declarative, interrogative, imperative, exclamations**.

ground   see under **figure and ground; tenor, vehicle and ground; common ground**

group nouns   These are nouns referring to groups of humans, such as *family, committee, team, government*, and so on. In English, such nouns have the peculiarity that they can show either singular or plural concord with a following verb:

The committee have/has decided to appoint a secretary.

The team has/have not won a single match this season.

Singular concord treats the group as a unit; plural concord treats the group as a collection of individuals. Hence, things that are true only of individual members of the group need plural concord: *The team are/*is wearing badges*. Conversely, things that are true only of the group as a whole need singular concord: *This committee was/*were set up last year*.

H

habitual   A habitual reading of a verb is one in which an event is construed as occurring on a more or less regular basis on different occasions. It is frequently signalled in English by the simple present tense: *Liz has a boiled egg for breakfast*. (Compare **iterative**.)

hedge   An expression which weakens a speaker's commitment to some aspect of an assertion:

> She was wearing **a sort of** turban.
> **To all intents and purposes**, the matter was decided yesterday.
> I've **more or less** finished the job.
> **As far as I can see**, the plan will never succeed.
> She's quite shy, **in a way**.

hierarchies (lexical)   see **lexical hierarchies**

holistic theories of word meaning   see under **atomistic vs holistic theories of word meaning**

holonym   see under **meronymy**

homograph   see under **homonymy**

homonymy, homonym   Homonymy occurs when unrelated meanings are signalled by the same linguistic form, as with *bank* ('side of river') and *bank* ('financial institution'): the two *bank*s are said to be 'homonyms'. Dictionaries usually treat these as different words and give them different main headings. If two meanings are associated with the same written form but different spoken forms, they may be called 'homographs' (e.g. *lead* (the metal) and *lead* (to guide)); if they are pronounced the same, but have different written forms, they are 'homophones' (e.g. *lead* (metal) and *led* (past tense of *lead*)). Prototypical homonyms are identical in both spoken and written forms. (Contrast with **polysemy**, where the different senses are related.)

homophone   see under **homonymy**

hyperbole   A figure of speech involving deliberate exaggeration for rhetorical effect, to increase impact or to attract attention. Exaggeration may be negative or positive. For instance, if someone says *He shot off like a rocket when I told him you were here* a (relatively) high rapidity of action is indicated, whereas *The traffic was moving at a snail's pace* exaggerates in the opposite direction. In neither case does the expression convey a literal truth, nor is it intended to deceive. Other examples: *She never stops talking, The toilets in this building are literally miles from my office, I wore my fingers to the bone putting up those shelves.*

hyperonym   see under **hyponymy**

hyponymy, hyponym   Hyponymy is the asymmetrical relation of sense between, for instance, *dog* and *animal* and between *daffodil* and *flower*. This relation is usually explained in terms of inclusion, but there are two ways of looking at this. Thinking of categories of things in the world (the **extensional** perspective), the category of animals includes the category of dogs, so that if something is a dog it is necessarily an animal. But thinking of meanings (the **intensional** perspective), the meaning of *dog* includes the meaning of *animal*. The term in a relation of hyponymy associated with the more inclusive category (*flower*, *animal*) is called the 'hyperonym' (also often called the 'superordinate') and the included category (*daffodil*, *dog*) is the 'hyponym'. Notice that a word may be a hyponym of one word and a hyperonym of another: *dog* is a hyponym of *animal*, but a hyperonym of *collie*. (Hyponymy must be distinguished from the other main relation of inclusion, namely, **meronymy**.) It is common for a hyperonym to have a set of incompatible hyponyms. This is the basis of a **taxonomic hierarchy**:

Hyperonym	Hyponyms
animal	*dog, cat, cow, camel, lion, giraffe, ...*
fruit	*apple, orange, banana, plum, ...*
tree	*oak, ash, yew, pine, sycamore, willow, ...*

I

iconic signs   see under **arbitrary vs iconic signs**

identity constraint   see under **identity test**

identity test   The identity test is one of the so-called ambiguity tests (see under **ambiguity**), designed to determine whether a word is truly ambiguous or merely has a **hyperonymic** meaning which can be narrowed down in different ways in different contexts. The usual form of the test utilises verb-phrase anaphora, as in the classic example: *Liz was wearing a light coat; so was Sue*. Here, the second conjunct (*so was Sue*) picks up the verb-phrase from the first conjunct and is interpreted as 'Sue was also wearing a light coat'. The adjective *light* has two meanings, 'light in colour' and 'light in weight'. But there is a restriction on the possible combinations of readings for *light* in *Liz was wearing a light coat; so was Sue*: whichever reading is chosen in the first conjunct must be retained in the second. That is to say, it is not possible for Liz's coat to be light in colour and Sue's light in weight (or vice versa). This is known as the 'identity constraint'. The presence of an identity constraint is taken as evidence for ambiguity. The above case may be contrasted with, for example, *Liz invited a friend; so did Sue*. Friends may be male or female, but there is no requirement for Sue's friend to be of the same sex as Liz's. Hence, the word *friend* is not ambiguous between 'male friend' and 'female friend'.

idiom   The term 'idiom' is usually applied to multi-word phrases, although theoretically words consisting of more than one morpheme can exhibit similar properties. Prototypical idioms have two principal characteristics: they are **non-compositional**, and they are syntactically frozen. Idioms are non-compositional in the sense that their global meanings cannot be predicted on the basis of any stable readings that their constituents may have in other contexts. A standard (extreme) example is *to pull someone's leg*. It is not possible to construct the meaning of this expression on the basis of standard readings of *pull* and *leg*. The expression *to pull someone's leg* is also syntactically frozen. For instance, the element *leg* is ostensibly a noun, but it cannot be modified in the usual way by adjectives, nor can it be pluralised, while retaining the idiomatic meaning: *Pete pulled Bill's left leg/injured leg, Pete pulled Bill's legs.* (Most idioms respect the rules of grammar. A few, known as 'asyntactic idioms', do not: an example is *by and large.*) For some idioms, knowing the usual meanings of the constituent words is of no help whatsoever in interpreting the idiom: *to pull someone's leg, spick-and-span, a white elephant, a red herring.* In other cases, the literal meaning is not totally unrelated to the idiomatic meaning. For instance, the meaning of *blackbird* has something to do with the meanings of *black* and *bird.* Many idioms are 'frozen metaphors', that is to say, metaphors that have become conventionalised and established: *all over the place, fall into place, have one's heart in the right place, know one's place, a place in the sun, keep someone in his place, go places, have friends in high places.* Syntactic frozenness is also variable. For instance, *to pull someone's leg* can be passivised: *Pete's leg was pulled continually,* but *to kick the bucket* cannot. *Place* in *know one's place* and *keep someone in his place* can be modified by *rightful* or *proper,* but in *all over the place, fall into place,* and *go places* no modification is possible without loss of the idiomatic sense. A distinction can be made between 'encoding' and 'decoding' idioms. Encoding idioms are **compositional**, but the meaning of one or more of the constituent words is idiosyncratic and not predictable from the **default** meaning. They typically cause non-native speakers problems in the production of correct forms, but fewer problems in comprehension. Examples are *answer the door* and *high wind* (these cases qualify as (one type of) **collocation**). Decoding idioms are **non-compositional**.

image metaphor   In the **Conceptual Metaphor Theory**, image metaphors are metaphors in which the **source domain** and the **target domain** are equally well structured, conceptually, in their own right (*Her eyes were dark holes, Icicles bared long teeth from the eaves* – both from the novelist Patricia Cornwell). In this, they differ from many conceptual metaphors (for instance, LIFE IS A JOURNEY), in which an abstract, less structured domain borrows structure from a more concrete, familiar and well-structured domain. Image metaphors are therefore less important as aids to reasoning and tend to have more of an aesthetic role, adding colour and feeling and moulding perception. Many literary metaphors are of this type.

image schemas   These are very basic conceptual elements which contribute to the construal of more complex conceptual structures. Examples are: the 'container' schema, which when applied to a category gives a boundary separating the inside from the outside; the 'centre-periphery' schema, which can also be applied to a category; the UP-DOWN schema (as in *Prices are up ten per cent*); the 'scale' schema; and the 'dichotomy' schema. When we describe a door as *either open or shut*, we use the latter schema, but when we speak of it as *wide open* or *slightly ajar*, we view the degree of opening of the door as a continuous scale.

immediate scope of predication   see under **profile and base**

impartiality (in antonyms)   see under **polar antonyms**

imperative   The prototypical function of a sentence in imperative form is to get someone to do something. The prototypical components of imperative meaning are

(a) an expression of the desirability of some state of affairs, (b) the belief that this state of affairs does not currently hold, (c) the belief that the addressee is capable of bringing about the desired state of affairs, and (d) the desire that the addressee should bring about the desired state of affairs. The grammatical imperative shares meaning with explicit **performative verbs** such as *command, tell to, urge, demand, request,* and so on, but is more general than any of them. The imperative also has non-prototypical uses such as *Show me a good loser and I'll show you a loser, Take another step and I'll shoot* and *Twinkle, twinkle little star.*

imperfective   see under **perfective vs imperfective**

implicatures   These are parts of the meanings of utterances which, although intended, are not strictly part of 'what is said' in the act of utterance, nor do they follow logically from what is said. There are two basic sorts of implicature: (a) those which have a stable association with particular linguistic expressions (**conventional implicatures**), such as the element of surprise associated with *yet* in *Haven't you finished yet?* (speaker does not actually say he or she is surprised), and (b) those which must be inferred, and for which contextual information is crucial (**conversational implicatures**), such as the implied negative in B's reply in:

A: Can I speak to Jane?
B: She's in the shower. Can you call back?

The study of conversational implicatures is a major sub-area within **pragmatics.**

inappropriateness   see under **anomaly**

inclusive first person forms   see under **person deixis**

inclusive vs exclusive disjunction   This refers to two interpretations of, for instance, the conjunction *or*. Take *or* in *The successful candidate will be a graduate or someone with managerial experience.* Clearly, someone who qualifies on both counts will not be excluded: this is the inclusive interpretation. The exclusive interpretation is illustrated by *Was the door open or shut?*

incompatibles, incompatibility   Lexical senses that stand in the relation of incompatibility denote mutually exclusive categories. For instance, if something is a dog then it cannot at the same time be a cat (equivalently, 'X is a dog' entails 'X is not a cat'); hence, *dog* and *cat* (in the relevant senses) are incompatibles. However, there is no entailment in the other direction: if something is not a cat, it does not follow that it is a dog, so *dog* and *cat* are not **complementaries**. All opposites are by definition incompatibles, but the most typical incompatibles form non-binary sets: *red*, *orange*, *yellow*, *green*, *blue*, *purple*, and so on; *circle*, *square*, *triangle*, *pentagon*, and so on; *car*, *lorry*, *van*, *bus*, and so on; *daffodil*, *crocus*, *tulip*, *hyacinth*, and so on; *hammer*, *chisel*, *saw*, *plane*, *screwdriver*, and so on. Incompatibility is a very important sense relation that must be distinguished from mere difference of meaning. For instance, *mother* and *teacher* are different in meaning but they are not incompatibles, since 'Liz is a mother' does not entail 'Liz is not a teacher'.

incongruity   see under **anomaly**

indefinite reference   This is when reference is made to some entity or entities, but the identity of the referent(s) is either not known or not relevant to the message being conveyed (compare **definite reference**):

There's *a man* at the door who wants to speak to you.
I can't find my wallet – I must have left it *somewhere*.
Come up and see me *sometime*.
He's *something* in the City.
She was run over by *a tractor*.

A distinction is usually made between 'specific in-definites' and 'non-specific indefinites'. Compare the following uses of *something*: (a) I hope he has bought me something nice for my birthday. (b) Come upstairs – I want to show you something. In neither case is the hearer required to identify the item referred to by *something*, so they are both indefinite. However, while in (a) the speaker gives no indication of having a specific item in mind, in (b) the speaker clearly has a specific item in mind. Notice that not all uses of the indefinite article involve indefinite reference. Some uses fall under **generic reference**: *A warthog is a gentle creature*. Other cases are not reference at all: *Liz is an artist*. This last sentence presents one of Liz's attributes, comparable to *Liz is tall*. It does not say that there is an artist in the world and Liz is that artist.

indexicality   For present purposes, indexicality can be taken as equivalent to **deixis**.

indirect speech act   This is an utterance that has the typical form of one kind of speech act, but which functions, either typically or in specific contexts, as a different type of speech act. Many instances of indirect speech acts are highly conventionalised. (This leads some scholars to maintain that their 'indirectness' is only of historical relevance.) The following are typical:

1. *You will do as I say* has the form of an assertive (i.e. makes a statement), but commonly functions as a directive (i.e. tries to get someone to do something).
2. *Would you mind if I opened the window?* superficially is a question inquiring about the hearer's attitude to a hypothetical event, but is a frequent way of requesting permission.
3. *Could you lend me a hundred pounds?* literally is a question regarding the hearer's ability to do something, but is conventionally used as a (relatively polite) directive.
4. *What did I tell you?* is literally a question, but conventionally functions as an equivalent to *I told you so!*

Other (so-called) indirect speech acts are probably best regarded as cases of **conversational implicature**, and perhaps do not deserve to be specially singled out. The following is an example:

Son: Dad, Mark and some of the lads are going bowling tonight.
Father: You're grounded. Remember?

The son's utterance has the form of a statement, and the father's consists of a statement followed by a question. But the son's utterance is understood as a request for permission, and the father's as a refusal.

individuative suffix   see under **plural**

inflection, inflectional affix   see under **affix**

information structure   see under **given vs new information, topic vs comment, foregrounding**

inherentness (in antonyms) see under **overlapping antonyms**

instrument, instrumental see under **functional roles**

intension see under **denotation**

intensifiers These are words or expressions which strengthen or weaken the degree of a property indicated by a **relative adjective** (or adverb). Examples are: *very, extremely, slightly, quite, rather, fairly, a little, a bit, on the X side*. *Very* and *extremely* strengthen the property (relative to the degree indicated by the bare adjective) and *slightly, a little, a bit* weaken it. (The latter three examples are more normal with negatively evaluative adjectives: *slightly/a bit/a little hostile/boring* vs *?slightly/a bit/a little friendly/interesting*.) The interpretation of several of these items depends on how they are pronounced. Compare the following (stress indicated by upper case): *This is QUITE SUPERB*; *Well, it was QUITE good*; *I thought it was quite GOOD*.

interrogative The prototypical function of a sentence in the interrogative form is to ask questions. A prototypical question expresses (a) a lack of knowledge on the part of the speaker (exam questions are atypical in this respect, in that the questioner already knows the answer), (b) a desire for the lack to be made good, (c) a desire for a response from the addressee that will fulfil (b), and (d) a belief that the addressee can supply such a response. (Not all languages have a distinct grammatical form for asking questions; some, like Turkish and Arabic, have an interrogative particle which transforms a statement into a question; other languages rely on intonation.) There are two basic types of question: 'Yes-No questions' and

'X-questions'. Yes-No questions effectively present a proposition and ask whether it is true or not. Thus *Is Pete here?* presents the proposition 'Pete is here' and expects the answer *Yes* if it is true and *No* if it is false. (Notice that in English, the question *Isn't Pete here?* receives the answer *Yes* if 'Pete is here' is true and *No* if it is false. This may seem obvious, but in some languages one must answer *Yes* to the equivalent question if 'Pete isn't here' is true and *No* if it is false.) In contrast, X-questions present a proposition with a term missing, and request an answer which fills in the gap to form a true proposition. Hence *Where is Pete?* presents the skeleton proposition 'Pete is –'; an answer *in the kitchen* means that the proposition 'Pete is in the kitchen' is true. (For questions functioning as requests for action, see **indirect speech act**.)

intransitive relations   see under **logical relations**

irony   A species of **figurative language**, in which the intended meaning of an expression is usually some kind of opposite of the literal meaning, as, for instance, when someone says *You've been a great help!* to a person whose actions or words have just precipitated a disaster. The literal meaning of an ironic expression typically echoes the words or assumed opinions of someone else, and is intended to mock or ridicule.

iterative   An iterative reading of a verb is one in which an event, usually a **punctual** one, is construed as occurring a number of times in close succession on a particular occasion. It is frequently signalled in English by the continuous form of the verb. For instance, a single cough is a punctual event, but in *Pete is coughing* the cough is understood as being repeated. (Compare **habitual.**)

L

landmark   see under **trajector and landmark**

langue vs parole   This is a distinction first drawn by Saussure, one of the founding fathers of modern linguistics, which had a profound influence on the development of the subject. It is basically a distinction between a language as an abstract system, which is the true object of the study of linguistics, and the use made of that system, in the sense of what speakers of the language actually say on particular occasions, which, for one reason or another, may not conform precisely to the underlying system. See also a related distinction between **competence** and **performance**.

latched turns   see under **conversational analysis**

latency   A latent element is one which must be recovered from context if an expression is to be understood properly. A good example is the direct object of the verb *watch* in, for example, *Pete was watching*. This is acceptable only if what Pete was watching is known or can be recovered from context. It is not true of all verbs that if their direct object is not mentioned it becomes latent. Although logically speaking Pete must be reading something, the direct object in *Pete was reading* is not latent. Notice that in *Pete was watching and so was Liz* both must be watching the same thing, but in *Pete was reading and so was Liz* there is no implication that they were reading the same thing. (Latency is also known as 'zero anaphora' or 'definite deletion'.)

Leibniz's law   see under **opaque contexts**

lemma   see **listeme**

lexeme   The fundamental unit of **lexical semantics**. It corresponds roughly to one of the everyday uses of the term 'word'. For a crossword solver, *talk*, *talks*, *talked*, and *talking* are all different 'words'; however, we would not expect to find separate entries and definitions for these in an ordinary dictionary, so from the perspective of a dictionary compiler they represent the same 'word'. It is the lexicographic word which corresponds most closely to a lexeme. Basically a lexeme is an association between form and meaning which ignores certain types of variation both on the form side and on the meaning side. On the form side, variations due to different **inflectional** affixes or processes are ignored, so *talk*, *talks*, *talked*, and *talking* are all considered to represent the same lexeme. On the other hand, **derivational** processes and affixes give rise to new lexemes, so, for instance, *obey* and *disobey* belong to different lexemes. (Notice that a lexeme is not the same as a root: *dog* and *cat* represent both different lexemes and different roots, but *obey* and *disobey* have the same root.) On the meaning side, things are slightly more complex. Opinions differ regarding the relationship between **senses** and lexemes. On one view, every different sense represents a different lexeme; on another view, **polysemous** senses belong to the same lexeme but **homonyms** belong to different lexemes; a third view is that all senses associated with the same form (or set of inflectionally related forms) belong to the same lexeme. These differences are a matter of convention rather than deep theoretical disagreement. Probably the second of the above characterisations is the most common: it corresponds most closely to lexicographic practice. Most scholars consider non-compositional **idioms** such as *a red herring* and *to pull someone's leg* as lexemes because of their semantic unity.

lexical decomposition   The analysis and description of word meanings in terms of **semantic components**.

lexical field   see under **structural semantics**

lexical gap   This term is applied to cases where a language might be expected to have a word to express a particular idea, but no such word exists. It is not usual to speak of a lexical gap when a language does not have a word for a concept that is foreign to its culture: we would not say, for instance, that there was a lexical gap in Yanomami (spoken by a tribe in the Amazonian rainforest) if it turned out that there was no word corresponding to *modem*. A lexical gap has to be internally motivated: typically, it results from a nearly-consistent structural pattern in the language which in exceptional cases is not followed. For instance, in French, most **polar antonyms** are lexically distinct: *long* ('long'): *court* ('short'), *lourd* ('heavy'): *leger* ('light'), *épais* ('thick'): *mince* ('thin'), *rapide* ('fast'): *lent* ('slow'). An exception to this is *profond* ('deep'), which has no single lexical item corresponding to *shallow*; instead, the French use the phrasal expression *peu profond*. An example from English is the lack of a word to refer to animal locomotion on land. One might expect a set of **incompatibles** at a given level of specificity which are felt to 'go together' to be grouped under a **hyperonym** (like *oak*, *ash*, and *beech* under *tree*, or *rose*, *lupin*, and *peony* under *flower*). The terms *walk*, *run*, *hop*, *jump*, *crawl*, *gallop* form such a set, but there is no hyperonym at the same level of generality as *fly* and *swim*. These two examples illustrate an important point: just because there is no single word in some language expressing an idea, it does not follow that the idea cannot be expressed.

lexical hierarchy   A grouping of lexical items whose meanings are related in a way that can be represented by means of a 'tree-diagram'. There are two main sorts of lexical hierarchy, which differ in respect of their constitutive sense relations. The first sort is the 'taxonomy' or 'classificatory hierarchy', in which the vertical relation is **taxonymy** (a variety of **hyponymy**) and the horizontal relation is co-taxonymy (a variety of **incompatibility**). Diagram 1 illustrates a portion of a taxonomy:

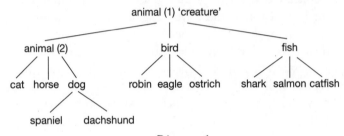

Diagram 1

The two occurrences of *animal* in Diagram 1 illustrate the phenomenon of 'auto-hyponymy', where one of the senses of a polysemous word is a hyponym of another sense. The items at a particular (horizontal) level in a taxonomy tend to have certain characteristics in common. (See **basic level, superordinate level, subordinate level.**) Diagram 1 shows four levels. Natural (i.e. non-technical) taxonomies rarely have more than five levels, although taxonomies of technical terms may have more. The second main type of lexical hierarchy is the part-whole hierarchy, or **meronomy,** in which the vertical relation is **meronymy** and the horizontal relation is **co-meronymy.** Diagram 2 illustrates a portion of a part-whole hierarchy:

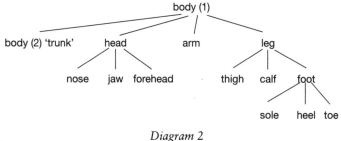

Diagram 2

The two occurrences of *body* in Diagram 2 exemplify 'auto-meronymy'. The levels in a part-whole hierarchy tend to be less significant than those in a taxonomy.

lexical meaning This is usually contrasted with **grammatical meaning**. It refers to the meaning of full lexical items such as nouns, verbs, and adjectives, which is typically richer and more complex than the meaning carried by grammatical elements such as affixes, prepositions, conjunctions, and so on.

lexical semantics The systematic study of meaning-related properties of words. Exactly what is included in the field is likely to vary from scholar to scholar, but central topics include: how best to specify the meaning of a word; **paradigmatic** relations of meaning such as **synonymy, antonymy,** and **hyponymy; syntagmatic** relations of meaning, including **selectional restrictions;** structures in the lexicon such as **taxonomic hierarchies;** change of word meaning over time; and processes of meaning extension, such as **metaphor** and **metonymy.** Lexical semantics is usually contrasted with grammatical semantics, and may exclude aspects of meaning treated under **pragmatics.**

lexical sense   A distinct meaning which has an established association with a given word-form is called a (lexical) sense. For a word-form to be described as having more than one sense, it must satisfy the criteria for **ambiguity**. Established senses normally have separate definitions in a dictionary.

lexicology   The systematic study of all aspects of words and vocabularies. It includes lexical semantics, morphology, phonological and graphological properties of words, etymology and processes of change over time, stylistic and literary aspects, lexical characteristics of authors, genres, types of discourse, dialects and registers, structures in the vocabulary, and typology of word structures. This grouping of fields of study is not common in the English-speaking world, but is well-established in mainland Europe.

listeme   Any item in an ideal lexicon of a language whose meaning cannot be predicted on **compositional** principles, and which must be learned individually. This includes **morphemes**, **lexemes** (including **idioms**) and, for some linguists, **phonesthemes**. This corresponds roughly to what lexicographers call a 'lemma'.

literal meaning   There are different uses of the notion of literal meaning. For instance, one might come across a statement to the effect that the literal meaning of *depend* is 'hang from'. It is true that if one traces the history of the word back far enough one will eventually find that meaning. But that is not one of the current meanings of *depend*. In linguistics, the term *literal* usually applies to one of the current meanings of a polysemous word. That meaning is likely to be (1) the **default meaning**, (2) a plausible source from which the other meanings can be derived, and (3) more 'basic' than the other meanings, that is, concrete rather than abstract, familiar rather than unfamiliar, or perceptual rather than conceptual. For instance, *grasp* can mean 'take hold of' or 'understand'. Using the criteria mentioned, we are more likely to choose 'take hold of' as the literal meaning:

1. If a foreigner or a child asks what *grasp* means, out of context, we are more likely to say 'take hold of' than 'understand'.
2. It is much easier to think of understanding as 'taking hold of something with the mind', than taking hold of something as 'understanding with the hands'.
3. A physical action is 'more basic' than a mental one.

litotes   see **understatement**

location, locative   see under **functional roles**

logical relations   If a predicate has more than one argument it can be said to represent a relation between the arguments. For instance, in 'A is above B', *(is) above* expresses a relation between A and B; in 'X is married to Y', *is married to* expresses a relation between X and Y, and so on. Logicians recognise two basic classes of relational properties which frequently crop up in linguistic semantics. The first is symmetry. Under this heading, there are two main types of relations: symmetric and asymmetric.

1. Symmetric relations: Suppose we express a relation R holding between two arguments x and y as xRy. If R is a symmetric relation, then if xRy is true so is yRx and vice versa. For instance, if 'X is married to Y' is true so is 'Y is married to X' and vice versa,

hence, *is married to* is a symmetric relation. Further examples of symmetric relations include: *is sitting next to*, *is the same age as*, *is a sibling of*.

2. Asymmetric relations: If R is an asymmetric relation, the truth of xRy guarantees the falsity of yRx and vice versa. For instance, *is taller than* is an asymmetric relation: if 'X is taller than Y' is true, then 'Y is taller than X' is false. Further examples of asymmetric relations include: *is the mother of*, *is a kind of*, *is a part of*, *outranks*, and so on.

The second class of relational properties is transitivity (NB: logical transitivity is different from grammatical **transitivity**). Again, there are two types of relation: transitive and intransitive.

1. Transitive relations: If a relation R is transitive, then the truth of aRb and bRc guarantees the truth of aRc. For instance, the truth of 'Pete is older than Liz' and 'Liz is older than Jenny' guarantees the truth of 'Pete is older than Jenny'. Further examples of transitive relations include: *is a* (a collie is a dog, a dog is an animal, therefore a collie is an animal), *is a descendant of*, *has precedence over*, and so on.

2. Intransitive relations: If a relation is intransitive, then the truth of aRb and bRc guarantees the falsity of aRc. For instance, if 'Liz is Sue's mother' and 'Sue is Jenny's mother' are both true, then 'Liz is Jenny's mother' is false. Further examples of intransitive relations include: *is the immediate superior of*, *is the day following*, and so on.

M

markedness   This is a notion particularly associated with structural linguistics. It refers to a type of asymmetry between the terms of an opposition, with one term being 'marked' and the other 'unmarked'. There are several interpretations of the notion of markedness; the main ones are as follows (they are not mutually exclusive):

1. Formal markedness: the marked term is signalled by the presence of a morphological 'mark'; the unmarked term is signalled by the absence of a mark. Examples are: *accurate* (unmarked): *inaccurate* (marked); *mount* (unmarked): *dismount* (marked); *lion* (unmarked): *lioness* (marked).

2. Semantic markedness: the unmarked term has an interpretation where the contrast between the terms is inoperative or 'neutralised'. For example, *a group of lions* may include both males and females, but *a group of lionesses* has only females, hence *lion* is unmarked and *lioness* is marked. We may speak of the *accuracy* of a measurement that we know to be *inaccurate*, but not of the *inaccuracy* of a measurement we know to be *accurate*; *How long is it?* is neutral with regard to the expected answer, whereas *How short is it?* assumes the answer will lie in the range of *short*, hence *accurate* and *long* are unmarked.

3. Distributional markedness: the unmarked term occurs in a wider range of contexts than the marked term. Consider the case of *Are your parents alive?* vs *Are your parents dead?* Both of these are normal when there are reasonable grounds for supposing the answer to be *Yes*, but only the former is normal as an open-minded question. Hence *alive* is distributionally unmarked.

The three types of markedness frequently go together, but not always. For instance, *prince* and *princess* show formal markedness, with *princess* being marked and *prince* unmarked. But neither of these has a use in which the contrast is neutralised, so there is no semantically unmarked term. Also, semantic markedness entails distributional markedness, but not vice versa: for instance, the contrast between *alive* and *dead* is never neutralised. Oppositions, like that between *hot* and *cold*, where neither term is unmarked, are described as 'equipollent'.

marked term (of opposition)   see under **markedness**

mass nouns   see under **countability**

material implication   A **proposition** P materially implies a second proposition Q if it is not (logically) possible for P to be true and Q false. This clearly includes the case where P **entails** Q. But there is a crucial difference between entailment and material implication: the former depends on meaning, whereas the latter depends solely on truth values. For this reason, material implication includes cases where there is no entailment. For instance, take the case of P = 'Felix sat on the mat' and Q = 'Bachelors are unmarried'. Clearly, P does not entail Q. But since Q is an **analytic proposition** it can never be false. Hence, it is never the case that P is true and Q is false, so P materially implies Q. This relation is of limited utility (compared with entailment) in semantic analysis, but it is important in logic.

maxims of conversation   These spell out in greater detail the consequences of the **Co-operative Principle**. In the original formulation by Grice there are four of these: Maxim of Quantity, Maxim of Quality, Maxim of

Relation, and Maxim of Manner. They are rules of conversational conduct that people do their best to follow, and that they expect their conversational partners to follow. They have a rational basis, and are not matters of pure convention (think the Highway Code rather than table manners).

1. Maxim of Quantity: this deals with the amount of information presented. It comprises two submaxims:
    (a) Make your contribution as informative as is required for the current purposes of the talk exchange in which you are engaged.
    (b) Do not make your contribution more informative than is required.
In most situations there is a 'happy medium' between saying too little and saying too much. For instance, if one has to give one's age, it is not usually enough to say *several decades*; but equally it would not be normal to say *thirty-seven years, three months, seventeen days, eight hours and twenty-seven minutes*, however accurate that might be.
2. Maxim of Quality: this has to do with truth-telling:
    (a) Do not say what you believe to be false.
    (b) Do not say that for which you lack adequate evidence.
There are many occasions when this maxim seems not to be followed (see, for instance, under **politeness**), but it is arguable that it represents a valid default position, that is to say we do not depart from it without good reason.
3. Maxim of Relation: This is simple and straightforward:
    Be relevant.

The truth of a statement is no guarantee that it is an appropriate contribution to a conversation: it must also connect suitably with the rest of the conversation. (According to some scholars, a suitable version of this maxim renders the others unnecessary: see under **Relevance Theory**.)

These three maxims can be combined into one: make the strongest statement that can relevantly be made that is justifiable by your evidence.

4. Maxim of Manner: This comprises four sub-maxims:
    (a) Avoid obscurity.
    (b) Avoid ambiguity (this means 'ambiguity in context').
    (c) Avoid unnecessary prolixity (i.e. excessive wordiness).
    (d) Be orderly (this means that if time relations are not explicitly expressed, events should be related in the order in which they occur).

For discussion of how the maxims help to explain **conversational implicatures**, see under **standard implicatures** and **flouting the maxims**.

meaningfulness This term can be interpreted in two ways. First, it can refer to the amount of meaning an expression has. On this interpretation, a more specific expression has more meaning than a more general one. For instance, *dog* can be said to have more meaning than *animal* because the meaning of *animal* is included in that of *dog*. Generally speaking, the more meaning an expression has, the greater the contextual restrictions on its use. Second, the term can refer to whether a phonetic (or graphic) sequence has meaning or not. For instance, in the word *disobey* the sequences *dis-* and *obey* both carry meaning, but *iso* does not. Meaningful sequences are generally expected to (a) be replaceable (including by zero), giving a different meaning, and (b) to carry the same meaning in a range of contexts.

meaning postulates   These offer an alternative to **lexical decomposition** (see under **semantic components**) as a way of formalising structural relations between the words of a language, in particular **paradigmatic sense relations**. For instance, the relation of **hyponymy** between *horse* and *animal* can be expressed as the meaning postulate *horse* $\Rightarrow$ *animal*. This can be interpreted as meaning that if a proposition P^1 contains *horse*, then substituting *horse* for *animal* will produce a second proposition P^2 which is **entailed** by P^1. Hence, 'A horse kicked Pete' entails 'An animal kicked Pete'. In principle, all sense relations can be represented by meaning postulates:

incompatibility:	*apple* $\Rightarrow$ ~*banana; banana* $\Rightarrow$ ~*apple* (~ means 'not')
complementarity:	*dead* $\Rightarrow$ ~*alive; ~alive* $\Rightarrow$ *dead*
synonymy:	*begin* $\Leftrightarrow$ *commence*

On this approach, an account of the structural relations within the vocabulary of a language requires a set of basic meaning postulates together with rules for extending them. For instance, if $W^1 \Rightarrow W^2$, and $W^2 \Rightarrow W^3$, then $W^1 \Rightarrow W^3$ (for example given that *mare* is a hyponym of *horse*, and *horse* of *animal*, then it follows that *mare* is a hyponym of *animal*, so this fact does not need to be separately represented).

meiosis   see **understatement**

mental lexicon   This is the permanent store of known words in the brain of every speaker of a language. It contains information specific to individual words – semantic, grammatical, and phonological – needed to use the words appropriately. Each of us has a mental lexicon that is at least partly different from everyone else's because of our different experiences of language. No one has a stored knowledge of all the words in a language, and the information about known words may be incomplete. There are many theories regarding what is stored and in what form.

mental spaces   These were originally introduced by Fauconnier to explain a range of semantic phenomena mostly connected with reference. They are temporary, limited packages of conceptual content set up to assist understanding and guide action on particular occasions. Consider the following scenario. Pete and Liz, a brother and sister, are actors in a play. Pete plays the part of a policeman, Bill, and Liz plays the part of a prostitute, Polly. In the play, Bill arrests Polly. All the following can express true statements relative to this scenario:

> Bill arrests Polly.
> Pete arrests Polly.
> Pete arrests Liz.
> Bill is not Polly's brother.
> Bill is Polly's brother.

The 'mental spaces' approach handles this by setting up two distinct mental spaces, a 'reality space' representing the real world and a 'play space' representing the fictional world of the play. In the above case, the reality space contains Pete and his sister Liz, but no arrests occur; in the play space, two characters Bill and Polly exist who are not brother and sister, and Bill arrests

Polly. The at first sight puzzling validity of apparently contradictory statements illustrated above is explained by the existence of correspondences between the entities in the two spaces: Pete corresponds to Bill and Liz to Polly. These correspondences mean that entities in one space can be referred to by means of expressions which properly identify their correspondents in the other space. So, for instance, the real-life Pete can be referred to by means of either *Pete* or *Bill*. Mental spaces can be used to illuminate many other examples of reference. One of these is the difference between specific and non-specific definites, as in the well-known case of *Liz wants to marry a Norwegian banker*. Here we can set up a reality space and a wish space. In the wish space, Liz marries a Norwegian banker. In the specific interpretation, the reality space also contains a Norwegian banker, although Liz has not yet married him. In the non-specific interpretation, no actual Norwegian banker is present in the reality space. Mental spaces also play an important role in blending theory (see under **blending (conceptual)**).

mention   see under **use vs mention**

meronymy   This is the 'part-whole' relation, exemplified by *finger: hand, nose: face, spoke: wheel, blade: knife, hard disk: computer, page: book*, and so on. The word referring to the part is called the 'meronym' and the word referring to the whole is called the 'holonym'. The names of sister parts of the same whole are called 'co-meronyms'. Notice that this is a relational notion: a word may be a meronym in relation to a second word, but a holonym in relation to a third. Thus *finger* is a meronym of *hand*, but a holonym of *knuckle* and *fingernail*. (Meronymy must not be confused with **hyponymy**, although some of their properties are similar: for instance, both involve a type of 'inclusion', co-meronyms and co-taxonyms have a mutually exclusive relation, and both are important in **lexical hierarchies**. However, they are distinct: a dog is a kind of animal, but not a part of an animal; a finger is a part of a hand, but not a kind of hand.)

metalanguage vs object language   This concerns the use of one language to describe another: the object language is the language being described and the metalanguage is the describing language. The metalanguage may be the same as the object language, as in a monolingual dictionary. Or it may be modified in some way: learners' dictionaries often have a special restricted vocabulary for definitions. In a bilingual dictionary, the metalanguage is another natural language. Formal semanticists seek to develop a precise logical formalism to function as a metalanguage for natural languages.

metaphor   A variety of **figurative** (i.e. non-literal) use of language. What distinguishes a metaphorical use of an expression is the relationship between its figurative meaning and its literal meaning. Metaphor involves a relation of resemblance or analogy, although this is not explicitly stated (compare **simile**). Thus, if a writer in the financial pages of a newspaper speaks of *a headlong flight into bonds* (perhaps because of a collapse in share prices on the stock market) she is relying for her effect on correspondences between a lot of people running away from some physical threat to a safer place and the precipitate selling of shares and buying of bonds by large numbers of investors. We are invited to 'see something as something else', in this case to see the widespread selling of shares as a disorderly flight. The effect of this is to highlight some aspects of the situation and play down others. Metaphors start their lives as fresh creations. As time passes, however, they may settle down and become established in the language as conventionalised or 'frozen' metaphors. A novel metaphor is usually recognised as such by the fact that its literal interpretation is in some way odd, and this triggers a search for a figurative interpretation. Conventional metaphors typically do not have to be processed in a special metaphorical way – their 'metaphorical' meanings are permanently stored alongside their literal meanings and simply have to be 'looked up' in the **mental lexicon**. Metaphor is probably the most important aspect of the flexibility and creativity of language. (For further details see under **Conceptual Metaphor Theory, blending** theory.)

metaphorical entailments   This term is used in **Conceptual Metaphor Theory** to refer to patterns of reasoning in the **source domain** of a **metaphor** which carry over into the **target domain**. Take the conceptual metaphor ARGU-MENT IS WAR, which underlies expressions such as *to attack/undermine/shoot down one's opponent's arguments*. In a war, if one manages to put all the enemy's armaments out of action one wins the war; likewise, if one demolishes all of one's opponent's points in an argument, one wins the argument. Or take the LINEAR SCALES ARE PATHS metaphor, which allows us to say, for instance, that team A *is ahead of* team B in a league table, meaning that it has more points. Several aspects of the logic of paths carry across in the metaphor. For instance, if A is ahead of B on a path, then B can overtake A but not vice versa. Likewise, if Team A has more points than team B, then B can overtake A but A cannot overtake B. Similarly, if A is ahead of B on a path and B is ahead of

C, then it follows that A is ahead of C. The same logic applies to the metaphorical path of the league table.

metonymy A variety of **figurative** use of language. What distinguishes a metonymic use of an expression is the relationship between its figurative meaning and its literal meaning. Metonymy involves a relation of association. Take the example *England were beaten 4–3 by Germany*. In their default uses, the words *England* and *Germany* denote countries, but here they are used to refer indirectly to sporting teams representing those countries. Notice that, unlike **metaphor**, metonymy does not rely on a relation of resemblance or analogy. The sorts of associative relation which support metonymy are many and varied. The following are some illustrative examples (*X via Y* means that some entity X is referred to using an expression that normally refers to Y):

> WHOLE via PART: *I noticed several new faces tonight.*
> (This relation between part and whole, called synecdoche, is sometimes considered to be distinct from metonymy.)
> REPRESENTING ENTITY via REPRESENTED ENTITY: *England collapse.*
> POSSESSED ENTITY via POSSESSOR: *He's not in the phone book.*
> CONTAINED ENTITY via CONTAINER: *The kettle's boiling.*
> WOOD via TREE: *It's made of solid oak.*
> PLANT via FLOWER: *We prune the roses in March.*

microsenses The microsenses of a word are distinct readings that behave in some respects like ambiguous readings, but which, unlike the latter, can be subsumed under an inclusive reading. An example of a word with microsenses is *ball*. There are different sorts of ball, but in normal use only one of these is intended: *The ball hit the crossbar* (football); *The ball dropped just over the net* (tennis). A question containing a word with microsenses can be answered on the basis of the contextually relevant microsense, even if another microsense would require a different answer. Take the case of two boys playing football. They tire of the game and one of them picks up the football and says *Let's play tennis*. The other boy replies *Have you got a ball?*, to which the first boy says *No, I thought you had one*. Notice that on the basis of the hyperonymic reading of *ball* this answer is untrue because the speaker is holding a football, but on the basis of the microsense 'football' it is a true and normal answer. However, what distinguishes microsenses like those of *ball* from genuine ambiguous senses is the fact that they can be united in a **hyperonymic** reading without **zeugma**: *Pete loves any kind of game that is played with a ball*.

middle voice   see under **voice**

modality   It is first necessary to distinguish a purely logical (truth functional) notion of modality from a more linguistic notion which is concerned with a speaker's expressed attitude to an expressed proposition. Logical modality (sometimes called 'aletheutic modality') is concerned with notions of necessity and possibility and their interrelations. In traditional modal logic there are two 'modal operators', $\Box$ ('it is necessarily the case that …') and $\Diamond$ ('it is possibly the case that …'). These are interdefinable using the negative operator ~:

$\Box p = \sim\Diamond\sim p$

('It is necessarily the case that P' = 'It is not possible that not P')

'It is necessarily the case that bachelors are unmarried' = 'It is not possible that bachelors are not unmarried'

$\Diamond p = \sim\Box\sim p$

('It is possible that P' = 'It is not necessarily the case that not P')

'It is possible that Pete is in London' = 'It is not necessarily the case that Pete is not in London'

There are two main dimensions of (linguistic) modality. The first is 'epistemic modality', which is concerned with certainty or doubt, possibility or impossibility, in other words the speaker's attitude to the truth of the proposition. Consider the degrees of certainty expressed in the following:

It might be in the top draw.
It could be in the top draw.
It should be in the top draw – that's where I usually keep it.
It must be in the top draw, because I put it there myself.

The second major dimension is 'deontic modality'. This is the dimension of obligation, permission and prohibition:

You must do it.
You ought to do it – it's your duty as a father.
You should do it.
You may do it.
You needn't do it.
You shouldn't do it.
You ought not to do it.
You mustn't do it – it's against the law.

Modality can be expressed lexically, using expressions such as *likely, unlikely, probably, possibly* for epistemic modality and *be obliged to, have to, be free to,* and so on for deontic modality. It can also be expressed by means of modal verbs such as *must, ought, may, might,* and so on. It is a notable feature of modal verbs that they regularly have the possibility of either a deontic or an epistemic interpretation: *It must always be kept in the top draw* vs *It must be in the top draw because I put it there myself; You may stay in Manchester for the time being* vs *Don't make any plans, you may be in Manchester that weekend.*

modal operator   see under **modality**

modal value   It is possible to classify modal expressions as (1) high, (2) median, or (3) low value, according to the semantic effect of negating the modal as opposed to negating the proposition under the modal. This can be illustrated with *necessary, probable,* and *possible.*

1. *necessary*: *It is necessary to do this*
   negating the modal: *It is not necessary to do this* (weak)
   negating the proposition: *It is necessary not to do this* (strong)
   A marked difference of meaning. This pattern is diagnostic of a high value modal.
2. *probable*: *It is probable that Pete did it*
   negating the modal: *It is not probable that Pete did it* (medium)
   negating the proposition: *It is probable that Pete did not do it* (medium)
   Little difference of meaning. This is diagnostic of a median value modal.

3. *possible*: *It is possible that Pete did it*
negating the modal: *It is not possible that Pete did it* (strong)
negating the proposition: *It is possible that Pete did not do it* (weak)
A marked difference. This pattern is diagnostic of a low value modal.

modal verb   see under **modality**

Modesty Maxim   see under **Approbation and Modesty Maxims**

Montague semantics   A method of assigning semantic interpretations to the syntactic expressions generated by a Montague grammar (named after the American logician Richard Montague), which is a type of categorial grammar. These semantic interpretations are formulated in terms of a system of intensional logic in conjunction with **possible world semantics**.

mood   A set of verb forms indicating one of a range of functions. An important three-way distinction of mood is between **declarative** (also called 'indicative'), **interrogative**, and **imperative**. Many languages have a 'subjunctive' mood which can have a variety of uses. In French, for instance, it is used following certain expressions of necessity (*Il faut que tu vienne* ('You must come')) and desire (*Je préfère que tu vienne* ('I prefer you to come')). Less commonly, it is independently meaningful. In the following, the distinction is one of **modality**:

Je cherche quelqu'un qui connait le quartier (indicative mood: 'I'm looking for someone who knows the district')

Je cherche quelqu'un qui connaisse le quartier (subjunctive mood: 'I'm looking for someone who might know the district')

Some languages, such as Turkish, have a mood ('dubitative', 'reportative', 'evidential') for describing events one did not witness at first hand, and about which one is therefore less certain:

Ahmet öldü (indicative: 'Ahmet died' (I have first-hand knowledge))
Ahmet ölmüş (dubitative: 'I understand/they say/ apparently Ahmet died')

The conditional form of the verb is sometimes included under mood.

morpheme   The smallest grammatical element that carries an independent meaning. This includes lexical roots and **affixes**, and **closed set** free forms, such as prepositions and conjunctions.

N

natural gender   see under **gender**

natural kind terms   These are words referring to certain categories of things in the natural world, like *sky*, *cloud*, *water*, *silver*, *kangaroo*, *sand*, *maple*, *salt*, *air*, and so on. Such words are not generally thought of in terms of definitions – in fact most people would be hard put to it to come up with definitions, unlike, say, *puppy*, which most could define as 'young dog', or *bachelor* ('unmarried man'), *screwdriver* ('implement for turning screws'), and so on. Words whose meanings can be plausibly captured in a definition are sometimes called 'nominal kind terms'. Natural kind terms behave in some ways like proper names, and according to one influential theory their meanings are acquired in a similar way. For two people to communicate successfully using nominal kind terms they have to have the same notion of what the terms refer to. If one person uses *bachelor* to mean 'unmarried man' and another person uses it to mean 'drunkard', they will have trouble communicating. This is not the same with proper names. Suppose a number of people are introduced to someone called Pete. Some think Pete is an angel, some an android, some a 'normal' human male. These different notions do not prevent *Pete* being used by members of the group to refer successfully. Natural kind terms are similar. We might be inclined to say, for instance, that *(common) salt* means 'sodium chloride'. However, many people use the term *salt* perfectly successfully without knowing anything about its chemical nature, and some may have mistaken ideas. In some ways it would be more revealing to say that *salt* means 'the stuff we conventionally call *salt*', just as *Pete* is 'the person we call *Pete*'. (See under **possible world semantics** for natural kind terms as **rigid designators**.)

Natural Semantic Metalanguage This is a system of componential semantics especially associated with Wierzbicka. It utilises what is intended to be a universal set of semantic **primes** derived from the study of as wide a range of languages as possible. It claims that all aspects of meaning can be described in terms of a surprisingly small set of primes (originally only eleven, but the list has been somewhat extended since), all of which can be expressed linguistically. The following is a recent list of primes:

substantives	[I], [YOU], [SOMEONE], [SOMETHING], [PEOPLE]
determiners	[THIS], [THE SAME], [OTHER], [SOME]
augmentor	[MORE]
quantifiers	[MORE], [TWO], [MANY, MUCH], [ALL]
mental predicates	[THINK], [KNOW], [WANT], [FEEL], [SEE], [HEAR]
non-mental predicates	[MOVE], [THERE IS], [(BE) ALIVE]
speech	[SAY]
actions and events	[DO], [HAPPEN]
evaluators	[GOOD], [BAD]
descriptors	[BIG], [SMALL]
time	[WHEN], [BEFORE], [AFTER], [A LONG TIME], [A SHORT TIME], [NOW]
space	[WHERE], [UNDER], [ABOVE], [FAR], [NEAR], [SIDE], [INSIDE], [HERE]
partonomy	[PART (OF)]
taxonomy	[KIND]
metapredicates	[NO], [CAN], [VERY]
interclausal linkers	[IF], [BECAUSE], [LIKE]
imagination and possibility	[IF … WOULD], [MAYBE]
words	[WORD]

The following is a typical analysis (from Wierzbicka 1996):

X feels frustrated:
X feels something
sometimes a person feels something like this:
    I want to do something

> I can do it
> after this, this person thinks something like this:
>> I can't do it
> this person feels something bad because of this
> X feels like this

Unlike many componential analyses, a Wierzbickan analysis does not in general allow logical or relational properties to be inferred.

natural vs conventional signs   Conventional signs are those which are established for communicative use in some community and which have to be specially learned (and often taught). Linguistic signs are obvious examples; so are traffic signs and the like. There are two interpretations of 'natural' in respect to signs. According to one interpretation, natural signs are based on causal connections in the natural world. In this sense we say that smoke is a sign of fire and dark clouds are a sign of rain. According to another interpretation, natural signs are signs produced by communicating beings that do not have to be learned but are instinctive, like animal cries and human signs such as smiling, weeping, and gasping.

near-synonymy   see under **synonymy**

negation   Negating a proposition has the effect of reversing its truth value. So, to take a simple case, if 'Pete is here' is false, then 'Pete is not here' is true, and if 'Pete is here' is true, then 'Pete is not here' is false. In more complex cases, the question of the **scope** of the negative can arise, as in 'Pete did not go to town and buy wine'. This means that 'Pete went to town and bought wine' is false. But this could be because (a) Pete did not go to town (but still bought wine), (b) he went to town but did not buy wine, or (c) he neither went to town nor did he buy wine. The sentence 'Pete has not recently stopped smoking' means that 'Pete has recently stopped smoking' is false. But this could be because (a) Pete has never smoked, (in which case the **presupposition** of *stop* is included in the scope of the negative), (b) Pete stopped smoking a long time ago (in which case only *recently* is in the scope of the negative), or (c) Pete has never stopped smoking (in which case the presupposition that Pete smoked is not within the scope of the negative). According to one influential view, these variant interpretations are not to be regarded as cases of **ambiguity** but are contextual specifications of the general negative, which simply asserts that the positive form of the proposition is false.

negative affixes   The main negative affixes in English are the prefixes *un-*, *dis-*, *de-*, *mis-*, *non-*, and *in-* (and its variants as in *impossible*, *illegal*, *irregular*) and the suffix *-less* (perhaps *-free* might be added here). The semantic effects of adding a negative affix are somewhat various, and the meaning of a particular affix often varies according to the stem to which it is attached. The following illustrate the main effects of negative prefixation:

1. logical negation: e.g. *possible: impossible, biological: non-biological*. 'It is impossible' is logically equivalent to 'It is not true that it is possible'.
2. polar negation: *like: dislike*. Notice that 'I dislike him' is not equivalent to 'It is not true that I like him', since the latter, but not the former, allows for the possibility of indifference.
3. reversive negation: *dress: undress, mount: dismount, contaminate: decontaminate* (see discussion of **reversive** opposites).
4. privative negation: *de-louse, de-ice*.

    5. evaluative negation: *understand: misunderstand, inform: misinform, spell: misspell*; also *polite: impolite, kind: unkind.*

negative polarity items (negpols)   These are items like *any, anything, anybody, anywhere, ever,* which occur in certain negative environments but not in the corresponding affirmative environments (at least not with the same meaning):

> *I haven't seen anybody/anything.*
> **I have seen anybody/anything.*
> *Nobody has ever done that before.*
> **Somebody has ever done that before.*
> *I don't have any money.*
> **I have any money.*
> *I haven't been anywhere.*
> **I have been anywhere.*

Notice also cases like: *I shan't stay long* vs **I shall stay long*; *I didn't say a word* ('I didn't speak') vs *I said a word ('I spoke'). Negpols also typically occur normally with interrogatives and conditionals:

> *Have you seen anybody/anything?*
> *If you see anybody going in, let me know.*
> *Is there anywhere you would like to go?*
> *Have you ever been to Egypt?*

neutralisation   see under **markedness**

non-compositional expressions   see under **compositionality**

non-coreferential anaphora   see under **anaphora**

non-natural vs natural meaning (meaning_{nn})   Non-natural meaning is meaning intentionally conveyed in an act of communication where the recipient of the message recognises the sender's intention to transmit it. Grice's definition of this runs as follows:

S *means*$_{nn}$ p by uttering U to A if and only if S intends:
   a. A to think p.
   b. A to recognise that S intends (a).
   c. A's recognition of S's intending (a) to be the prime reason for A thinking p.

This definition has been discussed primarily in connection with linguistic communication, but it can be generalised if we substitute something like 'producing a signal' for 'uttering U'. The following examples illustrate natural meaning:

Dark clouds mean rain.
Pete has left his keys on the hall table, which means he won't be able to get in tonight.
Pete's speech is slurred. That means he is drunk.

Most animal communication is likewise excluded from non-natural meaning.

non-propositional meaning   see under **propositional meaning**

non-transitive relations   see under **logical relations**

number system   Many languages have grammatical number, that is, a system of grammatical choices – most commonly inflections on nouns – that depend on how many of something is being referred to, as in *the book* (a single referent) and *the books* (more than one referent). A number system has at least two terms, **singular** and **plural**, and may additionally have a **dual**, a **paucal** or a

trial. All languages have ways of indicating 'how many', but some do it by purely lexical means, equivalent to *one book*, *two book*, *seventeen book*, *a few book*, *several book*, *many book*, and so on. This does not constitute a number system. A number system is not the same as a numeral system, which is a set of lexical expressions like *one*, *two*, *three*, *four*, *twenty-nine*, and so forth, with distinctive grammatical properties indicating exact numbers.

O

onomatopoeia   see under **arbitrary vs iconic signs**

ontological types   see **basic ontological types**

opaque contexts   Referentially opaque contexts are those in which Leibniz's law does not hold. This law states that substituting an expression in a declarative sentence for another expression with the same **extension** does not affect the **truth conditions** of the sentence. For instance, at the time of writing, the expressions *Tony Blair* and *the prime minister of Britain* have the same extension, that is, they refer to the same person. Leibniz's law states that if, for instance, *Tony Blair is tall* expresses a true proposition, then so does *The British prime minister is tall*, and so on. In certain contexts (opaque contexts), however, this type of substitution does not preserve truth conditions. Consider, for example, *Pete believes Tony Blair is tall* and *Pete believes the British prime minister is tall*. Suppose that Pete thinks that Charles Kennedy (not a tall man) is the British prime minister – in that case the two sentences will have different truth conditions. Typical verbs that create opaque contexts are those of 'propositional attitude', such as *believe*, *want*, *doubt*, and *hope*.

open set items   These are **morphemes** that have the following characteristics:

1. They typically belong to large substitution sets; that is to say, there is a relatively large choice of elements that can replace them in a sentence without affecting the grammaticality of the sentence.
2. There is a relatively rapid turnover in the membership of the substitutions sets with new members being added and others falling out of use, the changes being noticeable within the lifetime of a single speaker.
3. All full lexical items (nouns, verbs, adjectives, and some adverbs) contain at least one open set item (known as the 'root'), either alone or with one or more **affixes**. For instance, the word *dog* consists only of a root, but *disobeyed* has one root, *obey*, and two affixes, *dis-* and *-ed*. Most words have only one root; the exceptions, such as *timetable*, *greenhouse*, and so on, are known as 'compound words'.
4. They carry the bulk of the meaning of sentences.

opposite directions   see under **directional opposites**

oppositeness (lexical) (also frequently called 'antonymy'). The sense relation of oppositeness is a special variety of **incompatibility** involving a binary contrast. That is to say, opposite meanings represent a two-way division of some inclusive notion. The feeling of oppositeness is strongest if the 'two-ness' is somehow logically necessary. For instance, there are only two vertical directions, so *up* and *down*, *rise* and *fall* and *top* and *bottom* are 'good' opposites. Similarly, there are only two ways of changing one's marital status – one can get *married* or get *divorced*; there only two ways of deviating from average length – something can be either *long* or *short*. And so on. Sometimes a domain happens to have only two members without this being a logically necessary restriction. Think of the domain of buses, which is divided into *single-deckers* and *double-deckers*. In such cases the feeling of oppositeness, if present at all, is typically weak. There are various types of lexical opposite: see **complementaries**, **antonyms** (2), **directional opposites**, **converses**, **reversives**.

orientation   This usually refers to the UP-DOWN relation. In a small number of situations we have a choice as to which direction we take as UP when we describe something. For instance, if Pete is lying on the ground with one leg in the air and a beetle is moving along his leg towards his foot, we can say either that the beetle is going up Pete's leg or that it is going down, depending on whether we choose an orientation based on the inherent properties of Pete's leg (legs prototypically point downwards) or based on gravity. Where words such as *up*, *down*, *high*, *low*, and so on have a non-spatial reference, as in *Prices are high / are going up*, an increase in some quantity is usually associated with *up* and a decrease with *down*.

ostensive definition   A definition produced by pointing to one (or more) examples of X and saying *That is (an) X*.

overhearer   see under **speech event participant**

overlapping antonyms   These form a sub-type of **antonym** (2). They typically exhibit an evaluative polarity (unlike **polar antonyms**, which are typically objective and evaluatively neutral), with one term expressing a positive attitude towards the referent and the other(s) a negative attitude: *good: bad*; *polite: rude, impolite*; *kind: cruel, unkind*; *clever: stupid*; *gentle: rough*. Another property that differentiates overlapping antonyms from polar antonyms is that the comparative of the positive term is **impartial** but the comparative of the negative term is **committed**: for one thing to be *better* than something else it does not have to be *good*; but to be *worse* than something else; it has to be *bad*. Questions show a similar asymmetry: *How good is it?* is open-minded; *How bad is it?* assumes that 'it' is bad. Many of the properties of overlapping antonyms can be explained if it is assumed that each term of a pair has its own scale; thus, there is a scale of 'goodness' and a scale of 'badness' which points in the opposite direction. In the case of overlapping antonyms, the scales partially overlap, hence their name. For instance, in the case of *good: bad*, zero on the scale of badness corresponds to the point representing 'neither good nor bad' on the scale of goodness. Another distinctive feature of overlapping antonyms is the phenomenon of 'inherentness'. Take, for instance, the comparative forms *better* and *worse*. For most nouns, saying *A is better than B* is equivalent to saying *B is worse than A*: compare *Pete's exam results were worse than Bill's* and *Bill's exam results were better than Pete's*. However, for certain nouns a statement containing *worse* does not have an equivalent with *better*: *Pete's crime was worse than Bill's* is not equivalent to **Bill's crime was better than Pete's* – although *less serious* would be acceptable. This peculiar behaviour of antonymous adjectives occurs when we are dealing with things that are inherently bad – that is to say, things like crimes, illnesses, droughts, famines, earthquakes, and shipwrecks, of which there are no examples which could be described as 'good'.

overlapping turns   see under **conversational analysis**

$\boxed{\text{P}}$

paradigmatic sense relations   see under **sense relations**

paradox   see under **anomaly**

paralinguistic signs   These are signs that necessarily or typically accompany speech, such as gestures, facial expressions, modulations of the voice, and so on, but are
not part of the linguistic system as such. A stricter interpretation would exclude signs which can function in
the absence of speech, such as a smile, and include only
those which either cannot be produced unless one is
speaking, like pauses or changes of voice quality, or
cannot be interpreted without reference to accompanying speech, like a gesture illustrating *It was this big.*

parole   see under **langue vs parole**

participant roles   see **functional roles**

particularised conversational implicatures   see **generalised
vs particularised conversational implicatures**

partonymy   see **meronymy**

passive voice   see under **voice**

paucal   A term in the **number systems** of some languages
which denotes 'a few' entities as opposed to one, two,
three, or many. All languages which have a paucal also
have at least a singular and a plural in their number
systems. (See also **singular, dual, trial, plural.**)

pejoration   see under **semantic change**

perfect   The perfect is often considered to fall under the heading of **tense**. But it is not a straightforward tense locating an event in time. Consider the difference between the following (sentence 2 is in the perfect):

1. Liz took the pills.
2. Liz has taken the pills.

Sentence 1 locates the taking of the pills at a definite time in the past and directs our attention to the past event. Sentence 2 also locates the event in the past. However, what is presented as relevant is not the time at which the event occurred, but Liz's current state as a result. A concise way of formulating the meaning of the perfect is to say that it expresses the current relevance of past events.

perfective vs imperfective   This is the most frequent distinction of **aspect** to be expressed grammatically in the world's languages. Basically, the perfective aspect presents an event as a completed unit with no relevant internal structure. The imperfective aspect, on the other hand, takes an inside view of an ongoing event, so that its internal structure can be relevant and carries no commitment regarding completeness. In English, the distinction is often signalled by the 'simple' vs 'progressive' form of the verb: *Pete watched his neighbour mow the lawn* (the mowing is viewed as a closed event without internal structure: the whole event is relevant, but not the way it unfolds in time); *Pete watched his neighbour mowing the lawn* (no commitment as to whether the mowing was completed; Pete's period of watching falls within the period of activity of the neighbour). Aspect and **tense** are essentially distinct, but certain languages which lack the morphological means to express tense distinctions (such as Arabic) can do so via the perfective: imperfective distinction. This is because a default assumption concerning a completed event is that it happened in the past, while the default assumption concerning an incomplete event is that it is ongoing and taking place in the present.

performance   see under **competence vs performance**

performative verb   A performative verb is one which designates a specific **speech act** and which, if used appropriately, counts as the performance of the speech act. For instance, saying *I promise to be careful* counts as a promise to engage in a particular course of action. Other examples of performative verbs are: *ask, beg, beseech, command, congratulate, deny, deplore, declare, implore,* and *warn*. Only certain forms of the verb count as performing the speech act, mainly first person simple present active and third person present passive. For instance, *I congratulate you on your promotion* and *Passengers are warned not to lean out of the windows* count as congratulation and warning respectively. But although *I promised to do it* and *He will promise to do it* refer to the performance of acts of promising, they do not count as promises. A performative verb in a performative use can typically be accompanied by *hereby*: *I hereby promise to pay the sum of one hundred pounds* (but *?I hereby promised to do it*). (Contrast this with *persuade*: persuasion is normally accomplished by means of language, but *?I hereby persuade you to hand over the goods* is not possible, hence *persuade* is not a performative verb.)

person deixis   Person deictics designate the basic roles in a speech event, namely the speaker ('first person'), the person(s) spoken to ('second person'), and the person or persons who are neither speaker nor addressee ('third person'). Person deictics include pronouns (*I*, *you*, *him*; *mine*, *yours*, *hers*; *myself*, *yourself*, *herself*), possessive adjectives (*my*, *your*, *her*), and verb inflections (Latin *amo*, *amas*, *amat*, 'I love, you love, he or she loves'). Personal pronouns can have singular and plural forms. A plural form may apply even if only one referent is designated, provided that the referent can be taken to represent a group. For instance, the first person plural *we* is normally produced by a single speaker who represents a group. Some languages have a different first person plural form according to whether the represented group includes both the speaker and the addressee ('inclusive' form) or the speaker and others, but not the addressee ('exclusive' form). In Pidgin, for instance, the inclusive form is *yumi* (in origin *you-me*) and the exclusive form is *mifella* (in origin *me-fellow*). First person plural pronouns refer directly to a plurality of speakers only in the case of choral speaking. Direct reference to a group is much commoner with second person pronouns (think of a teacher addressing a class), and is virtually the norm for third person plural forms.

personification   This is a near relative of **metaphor**, in which events, typically with obscure or complex causes, are portrayed as being caused by a human-like agent. In some cases, the actual agent is personified. For instance, a volcanic eruption may be presented as the act of an angry subterranean giant or a storm as the act of a vengeful, airborne fury. In some cases, as when death is personified as a coachman, reaper, or thief, it is not so much the cause of death (such as disease or famine) that is personified, rather the event itself.

phenomenal features   These are features of an entity that can be directly perceived by any of the senses (sight, hearing, taste, and so on).

phonesthemes   These are clusters of phonemes that seem to have an association with particular semantic domains. Examples are: *gl-* in words which designate light effects, such as *glow, glimmer, glitter, glisten, gleam*, and *sl-* in words which indicate something unpleasant, such as *slob, slut, slimy, slither, sleazy, slovenly*. They are not grammatical elements and have no contrastive value; nor are they **onomatopoeic** in the normal sense.

pleonasm   This is a type of semantic **anomaly** where some aspect of meaning is felt to be unnecessarily duplicated. For instance, in *?I kicked it with my foot* the *with my foot* is felt to be redundant because it contributes no extra meaning: 'with the foot' is an essential part of the meaning of *kick*. Likewise, in *?a female actress, female* is redundant because 'female' is adequately signalled by *-ess*. (Likewise *a new innovation, an illegal murder*, and so on.) Notice that *I kicked it with my left foot* is not pleonastic, because although *kicked* incorporates the idea of 'with the foot', the noun *foot* is necessary to allow *left* to be specified. Mere repetition does not necessarily lead to pleonasm. For instance, *That was very, very good* is not pleonastic because the second *very* makes a distinctive contribution to the meaning by heightening the degree of goodness expressed. Similarly, *Pete shrugged his shoulders* is not pleonastic, although there is nothing else one can shrug. The reason appears to be that there is a subtle difference of meaning between *Pete shrugged* and *Pete shrugged his shoulders*: the former directs attention to the meaning of the gesture, while the latter highlights the action itself.

plesionymy   see under **synonymy**

plural   A term in the **number system** of a language. Its meaning depends on the other terms in the system. In a two-term system like that of English it indicates 'more than one' of whatever is being counted; in a three-term system including a **dual,** like that of Classical Arabic, plural indicates 'more than two'; in a four-term system it will mean either 'more than three' or 'more than a few', depending on the meaning of the third term. Some languages have a more specialised type of plural, either in place of or alongside the more usual type. For instance, many nouns in Arabic have a 'distributive plural' which indicates a plurality of types of something rather than a plurality of individuals. For instance, the word *shajar* ('tree') is indifferent to the number of individual trees, but specifies that they are of one type; it has a distributive plural form *ashjaar*, which denotes a plurality of tree-types. Arabic indicates an individual tree by means of an 'individuative' suffix: *shajara*; this form has a 'normal' plural indicating a plurality of individual trees: *shajaraat*. Some languages have a 'collective' plural which indicates a number of individual entities which are associated together in some way, as with members of a family or houses in a village.

pluralia tantum   Grammatically plural nouns that have no corresponding singular form, such as *scissors*, *glasses* ('spectacles'), *tights*.

polar antonyms   Polar antonyms form a sub-type of **antonym (2)**. Examples are: *long: short, heavy: light, fast: slow, deep: shallow, thick: thin, large: small, strong: weak*. They denote relative values along a single dimension, like length or weight, prototypically measured in conventional units. Describing something as, for instance, *long* (e.g. *a long journey*) means that its length is greater than some assumed reference value (often an average for the type of thing being described), whereas *a short journey* is one that is less than the reference value. One of the terms of a pair of polar antonyms is positive with respect to the underlying scale and the other is negative, in that they denote, respectively, 'more of' or 'less of' what the scale measures (*long*, *heavy*, *deep*, *thick*, *large*, *strong*). Positive polar terms (also known as 'supra' terms) form impartial yes/no questions, that is to say, questions which are open-minded about where on the scale the likely answer will lie: *How long is the fence? How heavy is the box?* (Some scholars treat impartiality as a form of **neutralisation**, with, for example, *long* as the **unmarked term** of the opposition and *short* as the **marked** term.) Negative terms (also known as 'sub' terms) form committed questions where there is a presumption that the answer will fall within a certain range of values: *How short is the fence? How light is the box?* (both of these are odd for some speakers, but for those who find them acceptable they indicate an expectation of a short fence and a light box respectively). The comparative forms of polar antonyms are impartial for both positive and negative terms; something does not have to be short to be describable as *shorter than* something else, nor does something have to be heavy to be describable as *heavier*. (Compare **overlapping antonyms, equipollent antonyms**.)

polarity   This is displayed when one term of a binary opposition is described as 'positive' and the other as 'negative'. The most obvious cases are where one term carries a negative affix which the other lacks: *possible: impossible, happy: unhappy, obey: disobey, dress:*

undress, and so on. But other types of opposition are said to have positive and negative terms. The main ones are as follows:

1. Logical polarity is based on the principle that 'two negatives make a positive'. For instance, *It's true that it's true* is equivalent to *It's true*, but *It's false that it's false* changes polarity and is equivalent to *It's true*. From this we can conclude that *false* is the negative term and *true* is positive.

2. Quantity polarity applies particularly to **antonym** pairs, where the positive term indicates 'more of' some property and the negative term 'less of', as with *long* (positive) and *short* (negative).

3. Evaluative polarity is where the positive term expresses approval and the negative term disapproval, as with *good: bad*, *polite: rude*.

politeness   Insofar as linguistic behaviour is concerned, politeness is a matter of minimising the negative effects of what one says on the feelings of others and maximising the positive effects (known as 'negative politeness' and 'positive politeness' respectively). Politeness can also be either speaker-oriented or hearer-oriented. Speaker-oriented politeness involves not saying things about oneself that would place one in a favourable position relative to the hearer; boasting, for instance, is for this reason inherently impolite. Utterances which directly involve the hearer fall into the domain of hearer-oriented politeness. Leech proposes a general 'Politeness Principle': Minimise the expression of impolite beliefs. This principle both constrains and is constrained by the **Co-operative Principle**. Clearly, there are occasions when it is more important to convey relevant true information even if it has negative effects on the hearer. Like the co-operative principle, the politeness principle is expanded by means of a set of maxims (see the entries for **Tact and Generosity Maxims, Approbation and Modesty Maxims, Agreement Maxim, Sympathy Maxim**). There are, in addition, three minor principles:

Banter Principle: this allows us to be polite while being superficially rude, as when one says to a good friend *Look what the cat's brought in!* The underlying message is 'We are such good friends we don't need to be polite.'
Irony Principle: this allows us to be impolite while being superficially polite, as in *You should be very proud of yourself*, said to someone who has made a mess of something.
Pollyanna Principle: this enjoins us to avoid drawing attention to things 'which are not mentioned in polite company'. It is this principle which underlies the use and development of **euphemisms**. Politeness also enters into ways of addressing people. Many languages have a choice of pronouns for designating the addressee according to the relationship between speaker and addressee and, to some extent, the situation (these are sometimes called 'T/V pronouns'). Examples are French *tu/vous*, Italian *tu/Lei*, German *du/Sie*, and Turkish *sen/siz*. The exact conventions for using these forms differ from language to language, but we may take French as an example. We may first distinguish asymmetrical usage from symmetrical usage. Asymmetrical usage is relatively rare in modern French but it can still be observed in, for instance, a school setting, where pupils will address a teacher as *vous* and the teacher will address a pupil as *tu*. The distinction marks a difference of social status. In the more common symmetrical use, *vous* (sometimes called the 'polite form') marks either psychological distance (respectful or otherwise) or a formal situation (or both), while *tu* (the 'familiar form') indi-

cates intimacy/familiarity or an informal situation (or both). (The rules are quite subtle – the foregoing is a first approximation.) English does not use T/V pronouns, but, as in many languages, politeness enters into the choice of forms of address, such as *Pete*, *Smith*, *Mr Smith*, *Professor Smith*, *Sir Peter*, and so on.

polysemy A word which has more than one distinct, established **sense** is said to be polysemous (or to show polysemy). To be considered as belonging to the same word, multiple senses must be felt by native speakers to be related in some way. (Unrelated senses associated with the same word-form, such as 'side of river' and 'financial institution' associated with *bank*, exemplify **homonymy**, and are usually treated as separate words that just happen to be associated with the same form.) There are a number of relationships which may hold between polysemous senses. For instance, they may be related by **hyponymy**, as in the case of *drink* ('imbibe liquid' and 'imbibe alcoholic beverage') or *dog* ('canine animal' and 'male canine animal'). Several polysemous relations involve a contrast between **literal** and **figurative** meanings of a word. This may be **metaphorical**, as in *position* ('location in space', 'opinion on some controversial issue', and 'professional post within an organisation'), or it may be **metonymic**, as in *wheels* ('revolving parts of a mechanism in contact with ground' and 'car'), or it may involve **hyperbole**, as in *fantastic* ('so extreme as to challenge belief' and 'a generalised term of approval') (from *Longman Dictionary of the English Language*). Dictionaries usually treat homonymy and polysemy differently: homonymous readings are given separate main headings, while polysemous readings are typically distinguished by means of numbers under a single main heading. Some dictionaries make the distinction between homonymy and polysemy on etymological grounds, that is to say, meanings which have the same etymological origin are considered to be polysemous, even if modern speakers can intuit no relation between them, as in the case of *battery* ('infliction of blows', 'set of similar or connected cells'), both of which derive from the French *batterie*, while meanings which are usually felt to be related are treated as homonymy if they have different etymological origins, as in the case of *ear* ('organ of hearing' and 'grain of corn on stalk'). It should be pointed out that although the distinction between homonymy and polysemy is clear enough in extreme cases, the boundary between them is not very well defined. Not only is there a continuous scale of relatedness, but different speakers vary in their sensitivity to relationships.

possible world semantics   This is an approach to the semantic interpretation of logical formulae in certain systems of formal semantics, in particular those like the so-called **Montague semantics** that are based on **intensional** logic. The basic idea is that the actual world (in the broadest sense of everything existing) is only one of an infinite number of conceivable alternative worlds which differ in at least one respect from the actual world. Some possible worlds are very close to the actual world. For instance, there is a possible world identical to the actual world except that I did not mis-type the currant sentence. Others differ in major respects: for instance, there is one in which Napoleon was victorious at Waterloo. Others are hugely different, where, for instance, our galaxy does not exist. The following examples give a very brief idea of the sort of uses made of the concept of possible worlds (for a fuller understanding, more advanced works need to be consulted).

Extension and intension:
The extension of a noun like *dog* is the set of all dogs in the actual world.
The intension of *dog* is the set of all dogs in all possible worlds.
The extension of a sentence like *Dogs are animals* is its truth value in the actual world.
The intension of a sentence is its truth condition(s), interpreted as the set of all possible worlds in which it is true.

Analytic and synthetic propositions:
An analytic proposition is one which is true in all possible worlds.
A contradictory proposition is one which is false in all possible worlds.
A synthetic proposition is one which is true in at least one possible world.

Entailment:
P entails Q is true if in all worlds in which P is true, Q is also true.

Rigid designator:
A rigid designator is a term which refers to the same individual in all worlds in which that individual occurs. For instance, the term *eleven* designates the same number in all worlds where it has the same meaning as in the actual world. This may seem a tautology, but contrast *eleven* with *the number of gold medals won by Britain at the 2004 Olympics*, which also designates a number but clearly not the same number in all possible worlds. Proper names in general are held to be rigid designators, but **definite descriptions** are in principle capable of designating different individuals in different worlds without change of meaning.

pragmatics   Most linguists draw a distinction within the
study of meaning between semantics and pragmatics,
but there are several ways of drawing the distinction.
The main ones are as follows:

1. Semantics deals with **truth conditional** aspects
   of meaning; pragmatics deals with non-truth conditional aspects.
2. Semantics deals with context-independent aspects
   of meaning; pragmatics deals with aspects where
   context must be taken into account. Context is
   understood here in a broad sense that includes
   previous utterances (discourse context), participants in the speech event, their interrelations,
   knowledge, and goals, and the social and physical
   setting of the speech event.
3. Semantics deals with conventional aspects of
   meaning, that is, where there is an established
   connection between form and meaning. Pragmatics
   deals with aspects of meaning that are not 'looked
   up' but which are 'worked out' on particular
   occasions of use.
4. Semantics is concerned with the description of
   meanings; pragmatics deals with the uses made
   of those meanings. This is sometimes expressed by
   saying that semantics takes a formal approach and
   pragmatics a functional approach.

These different definitions have consequences in terms
of what is included in pragmatics, but there is a fair
measure of agreement that the following belong to
pragmatics: politeness phenomena, reference and deixis,
implicatures, and speech acts. Practitioners of linguistic
pragmatics have a preference for aspects of language use
which are amenable to broad generalisations, which are

language and culture independent, and which can be correlated with language structures.

predicate calculus (predicate logic)   This is one of the two main traditional systems of logic used in **formal semantics** (the other being the **propositional calculus**). In this system, **propositions** are analysed in terms of **arguments** and **predicates**. The simplest form of logical expression is a 'logical function' consisting of a 'constant', which functions as predicate, and one or more 'variables', which represent possible arguments. The following is a simple function:

DOG (x)

Here, 'x' is a variable, because it can take different 'values', which correspond to different entities in the world. Assigning a value to the variable in this expression yields a proposition, for example DOG (Fido), which translates into ordinary language as *Fido is a dog*. The element DOG is a constant corresponding to the meaning of the word *dog*. Predicate logic also uses a number of operators, which designate logical operations and relations and allow more complex expressions to be built out of simple ones. The most important operators are the existential operator '∃' ('for some ...') and the universal operator '∀' ('for every ...'), together with '&' ('and'), '⇒' ('if ... then') and '~' ('not'). The use of these is illustrated in the following:

(∀x)(DOG x)⇒(ANIMAL x)

This can be read as 'For all x, if x is a dog, then x is an animal' or, in more straightforward language, 'All dogs are animals'. In this formula, 'x' is a variable which takes as its value some entity; DOG and ANIMAL are constants representing the meanings of the words *dog* and *animal* respectively. The following exemplifies the use of the negative operator:

$$(\forall x)(\text{DOG } x) \Rightarrow \sim(\text{FLOWER } x)$$

This translates as 'For all x, if x is a dog, then x is not a flower' or 'No dogs are flowers'. The use of the existential operator is illustrated in the following:

$$(\exists x) (\text{MAN } x) \ \& \ (\exists y) (\text{DOG } y) \ \& \ (\text{SEE } x,y)$$

A strict translation of this (ignoring tense) runs as follows: 'There exists at least one x such that x is a man, and there exists at least one y such that y is a dog and x saw y'. Or, in ordinary language, 'A man saw a dog'.

predicate (logical)   see under **proposition**

predicative adjectives   see under **adjectives (order and placement)**

presupposition   A presupposition is a **proposition** whose truth is taken for granted by the producer of an utterance and which must be known and taken account of for the utterance to make sense to an interpreter. Take the case of *Pete has stopped smoking*. Someone using this sentence to make a bona fide literal statement takes it for granted that Pete was previously a smoker, although this is not explicitly stated. And the presumption that Pete had been a smoker is necessary for the sentence to make sense to a hearer, even if that fact was not previously known. Presupposition is not the same as **entailment**. Take a genuine case of entailment such as that between 'Pete killed the beetle' and 'The beetle died'. First, if we negate the entailing sentence, the entailment fails: 'Pete did not kill the beetle' entails neither 'The beetle died' nor 'The beetle did not die'. However, 'Pete has not stopped smoking' carries the same presumption as the affirmative version, as does 'Has Pete stopped smoking?'. Second, an entailment cannot be denied without contradiction: 'Pete killed the beetle, but it did not die' is a contradiction. A presupposition, on the other hand, can be denied (although it needs a special intonation): 'Pete HASN'T stopped smoking because he never DID smoke'. Presuppositions are ubiquitous. The following are some examples:

Utterance:	The flying saucer landed right here.
Presupposition:	A flying saucer landed. Flying saucers exist.
Utterance:	Liz regrets / does not regret selling the house.
Presupposition:	Liz sold the house.
Utterance:	Liz plays / does not play the bassoon brilliantly.
Presupposition:	Liz plays the bassoon.

There has been some dispute as to whether presuppositions are a semantic or a pragmatic phenomenon. If they are inherent properties of certain linguistic expressions then they are semantic in nature; if, on the other hand, they are a property of utterance(s)-in-context then they are pragmatic. Currently, the weight of scholarly opinion is in favour of a pragmatic analysis.

primary tense   see under **temporal deixis**

priming   This concerns a finding in experimental psycholinguistics. Subjects are asked to press either a 'Yes' or a 'No' button in response to a sequence of letters flashed on a screen, according to whether the letters form a word (e.g. BANK) or not (e.g. MANK). The time between the appearance of the letters and the pressing of the button is measured under various conditions. One of the conditions is the presentation of a word just prior to the test sequence. When the test sequence forms a word, it is found that if the preceding word is semantically related to the test word then the 'Yes' response is speeded up, whereas an unrelated preceding word has no effect. Suppose the test sequence is BREAD. The response to this will be faster if it is preceded by LOAF than if it is preceded by, for instance, LOAD. This speeding up is called priming. The closer the relationship between prime and test item, the greater the priming effect. Hence, both START and FINISH will prime BEGIN, but the former will have the greater effect. True semantic priming is dependent on the degree of similarity between meanings. It is usually distinguished from 'associative priming', which depends on how strongly two items are associated. For instance, BUTTER primes BREAD, but this is not due to resemblance between the two but to the fact that they frequently occur together.

privative adjective   An adjective that negates some essential feature of the noun it modifies. Examples are *fake*, as in *a fake Renoir*; *imitation*, as in *an imitation gun*; *reproduction*, as in *reproduction antiques*.

privative antonyms   Privative antonyms are a sub-type of **overlapping antonym**. Examples of this type are *clean: dirty, safe: dangerous, sober: drunk, accurate: inaccurate, satisfactory: unsatisfactory*. They exhibit the usual properties of overlapping antonyms. For instance, they show an evaluative polarity; one term is **impartial** in the comparative (*cleaner* does not presuppose *clean*) while the other term is **committed** (*dirtier* does presuppose *dirty*); and one term yields an impartial *how*-question (*How clean is it?*) and the other a committed question (*How dirty is it?*). They are distinguished from other members of the overlapping type by the fact that the evaluatively negative term indicates the presence of some undesirable property, while the evaluatively positive term indicates the absence of the undesirable property. Taking *clean: dirty* as an example of this type, the fact that *clean* is an 'absence' term can be appreciated from the fact that a definition of *clean* in terms of absence is much more natural than a parallel definition of *dirty*:

> *clean* 'something is clean when no dirt is present'
> *dirty* 'something is dirty when no cleanness is present'

privative opposition   see under **markedness**

profile and base   These notions are particularly associated with Langacker's approach to cognitive linguistics. They have a close relationship with the **frame semantics** approach to meaning, as well as the gestalt psychologists' notions of **figure** and **ground**. The basic idea is that a concept cannot be properly understood in isolation but needs to be seen as a highlighted portion ('profile') of a more inclusive conceptual domain ('base'). This can be seen most clearly in the case of things that are parts of other things. Take the case of FINGER. This 'profiles' a particular part of a HAND, and cannot be understood except against the background of the base HAND (HAND is known as the immediate 'scope of predication' of FINGER). The concept HAND is itself a profiled region of a larger base, namely, ARM, which in turn is profiled against the base BODY. (BODY represents the end of the profile-base chain, as it is not a profiled part of anything larger and can thus be termed the 'ultimate scope of predication' of FINGER.) FINGER, besides being profiled against HAND, can act as a base for profiled regions such as KNUCKLE and NAIL. Other examples of profile and base are: HYPOTENUSE-RIGHT-ANGLED TRIANGLE, PEAK-MOUNTAIN, MOUTH-RIVER (as well as e.g. MOUTH-BODY), NIB-PEN, and so on. A less obvious case is something like COUSIN, which represents a profiled relation in a network of relationships. COUSIN cannot be interpreted except against a base of relationships (perhaps representable as FAMILY) that includes at least PARENT, OFFSPRING, and SIBLING.

projected deixis   This is when **deictics** are used in their usual way, but the deictic centre is not the speaker but some other participant in the speech event, most commonly the **addressee.** For instance, the verb *come* has deictic properties in that its basic use is to denote movement towards the speaker, as in *Come here!* However, in *Shall I come and see you?* the movement in question is towards the addressee. In reported speech in English (but not in all languages) it is normal to project the deictic centre from the original speaker to the reporting speaker:

Pete (on Tuesday):   I'll go there tomorrow.
Bill (on Thursday):   Pete said he would come here yesterday.

pronouns   The main types of pronoun are personal pronouns (see under **person deixis**), demonstrative pronouns (see under **spatial deixis**), and **reflexive pronouns.** Pronouns may be definite (*I*, *you*, *this*, *that*) or indefinite (*something*, *somebody*). They may function anaphorically or exophorically (see under **anaphora**).

proper nouns   These are basically names of individual people (*Pete*, *Liz*), places (*Manchester*, *Switzerland*), works of literature, music, and art (*Pride and Prejudice*, *Finlandia*), dates and periods of time (*Christmas*, *February*, *Thursday*), and so on. In their basic use they are definite, in the sense that in context they refer to some identifiable individual entity. Thus *I saw Pete yesterday* does not just mean 'I saw someone called Pete yesterday', but also presupposes that the hearer can identify which particular Pete is being referred to. In certain contexts they are re-interpreted as common nouns, that is, nouns that denote a class or type of entity rather than a particular individual:

There are three Petes in the class.
The Pete you are looking for works in the library.
Oh, that Pete. No, he doesn't live here.

proposition   The simplest type of proposition consists of an **argument** (an entity about which something is 'said') and a **predicate** (what is 'said' about the argument). In the proposition 'Pete is tall', 'Pete' is the argument and '(is) tall' is the predicate. Some predicates need more than one argument to form a complete proposition: 'like', for instance, requires two ('Pete likes Liz') and 'give' requires three ('Pete gave Liz a present'). Predicates may be described as *one-place*, *two-place* or *three-place* according to the number of arguments they take. A proposition has a **truth value**, that is, it is either true or false. It is not a linguistic expression, nor is it tied to any particular linguistic expression. The same proposition may be expressed by different linguistic means, and a given sentence may be used to express different propositions on different occasions. So, for instance, *Pete is here*, *My brother is here*, *Liz's boyfriend is there* can very well express the same proposition, provided the same individual and place are designated, while *I am married* will express a different proposition for each different speaker. The proposition is what is asserted in a statement, what is questioned in a question (*Is Pete here?*) and what is denied in a negation (*Pete is not here*).

propositional attitude verbs   see **opaque contexts**

propositional calculus (propositional logic)   A system of logic which treats propositions as unanalysed atomic entities and examines systematic relations among them. This is one of the two main systems of logic used in **formal semantics** (the other being the **predicate calculus**). The logical relations between propositions are often displayed by means of 'truth tables', which show all possible combinations of truth values. For instance, the relation of **material implication** can be defined as follows:

P	Q	P$\Rightarrow$Q
T	T	T
F	T	T
T	F	F
F	F	F

In this table 'T' stands for 'true' and 'F' for 'false', as applied to the propositions P and Q and the expression P$\Rightarrow$Q. Hence, this table shows that the only relation between P and Q that rules out P$\Rightarrow$Q is if P is true and Q is false. The above pattern of truth values holds if, for instance, P is 'Fido is a dog' and Q is 'Fido is an animal'.

propositional meaning, content   The propositional content of a linguistic expression is that part of its meaning which determines its **truth conditions**. It thus excludes expressive meaning, evoked meaning and other aspects of **conventional implicature**, which all fall under the heading of non-propositional meaning. For instance, *Pete is here* and *Pete is still here* do not mean the same, but since they express true propositions in the same set of circumstances (that is, they have the same truth conditions), their propositional content is the same.

propositional synonymy   see under **synonymy**

prospective   The prospective can be seen as a mirror image of the **perfect**: the perfect expresses the current relevance of a past event, while the prospective expresses the current relevance of a future event. A straightforward future tense makes a prediction: *It will probably rain next week*; the prospective brings current readiness in terms of decisions, arrangements, and so forth into the picture: *I am going to take a few days' holiday next week*. Notice that *It's going to rain next week* suggests that we should do something about it now, such as change our holiday plans.

protasis   The clause in a conditional sentence (usually introduced by *if ...*) that states the condition under which the statement expressed in the **apodosis** is valid: *If you pay me what you owe me* (protasis), *I will take no further action* (apodosis).

prototype effects   The **goodness-of-exemplar rating** of an item within a category (that is, how close it is to the prototype) is correlated with a number of different properties. These correlations are known as prototype effects. The following is a selection of the main ones:

1. Order of mention: if experimental subjects are asked to name as many members of a given category as they can, more central members tend to be produced before more peripheral members.

2. Frequency of mention: if the responses of a large number of subjects in the above experiment are combined, it is found that the overall frequency of mention of a member of a category is correlated with its goodness-of-exemplar rating.

3. Priming: in **priming** experiments, the prior presentation of the category name speeds up recognition of all category members, but the effect is greatest for the prototype of the category. Hence, a prior presentation of *fruit* will speed up recognition of *apple* more than it will the recognition of, say, *date*.

4. Verification time: if subjects are presented with two names and have to say as quickly as possible whether or not the first is a member of the category represented by the other, responses are fastest if the first item is the prototype of the category. (For instance, subjects will answer 'Yes' more quickly to *apple: fruit* than to *date: fruit*.)

These effects are taken to show that goodness-of-exemplar ratings measure a psychologically significant characteristic of concepts.

prototype theory   This is a theory about the nature and structure of **concepts,** one of several proposals aimed at remedying the shortcomings of the **classical theory** of concepts (see also **exemplar theory**, the '**theory theory**'). The basic idea is that a concept is centred round a representation of an ideal example, or prototype. On this view, whether something belongs to a category and, if so, how central it is, are determined by its degree of resemblance to the prototype. In most versions of prototype theory, the prototype is represented by a set of features reminiscent of those found in the classical theory. For instance, the concept BIRD might be represented by the features [HAS FEATHERS], [HAS WINGS], [FLIES], [HAS TWO LEGS], [LAYS EGGS], [BUILDS A NEST], [SINGS], and so on. (This is sometimes described as a 'summary representation', because it does not contain details of individual examples.) The degree of resemblance of an item to the prototype is measured by the number of features it shares with the prototype. Some versions allow certain features to be more important than others. (Some prototype theorists interpret 'degree of resemblance to prototype' as 'degree of membership in the category'. On this interpretation, an ostrich would not be a full member of the category BIRD because it cannot fly.) The main differences between prototype theory and the classical theory are as follows:

1. The set of prototype features does not constitute a definition, as the features are not individually necessary. Membership of a category is determined by having a sufficient degree of resemblance to the category prototype, that is, by sharing a sufficient number of features. Many prototype theorists espouse the notion of **fuzzy boundaries**, believing that there is no sharp division between members and non-members of the kind entailed by the classical theory. Those who recognise boundaries define them as reaching a qualifying threshold of degree of resemblance.

2. Members of a category do not all have the same status: experimental subjects judge some members of a category to be 'better examples' (have a higher **goodness-of-exemplar rating**) than others. The classical theory offers no account of this.

3. The fact that not all features have to be satisfied means two members of a category may resemble the prototype in different ways and as a con-

sequence may have little resemblance to one another. This gives rise to the phenomenon of **family resemblance** as the unifying principle of category membership. (For more details see under **prototype effects**.)

psychological essentialism   see **essentialism (psychological)**

punctual   A punctual verb denotes an event that is thought of as happening in an instant: *The bomb exploded*, *Liz switched on the lights* (compare **durative**).

pun   A form of word-play in which two or more meanings of an expression are activated at the same time. Some puns involve **zeugma**: *He may well expire before his passport does*. But in other cases no actual anomaly is involved: *Some photographers decided to set up a focus group*. In some cases the ambiguous expression is repeated, as in Benjamin Franklin's famous example: *If we don't hang together, we'll hang separately*. Some puns involve different expressions with similar pronunciation, rather than two meanings associated with a single form: *That's a terrible cough you've got. Consumption be done about it?* (The second and fourth examples above were found at www.punoftheday.com)

pure vs impure deixis   A pure deictic element gives information only about the location of a referent relative to the speaker on some dimension, but gives no descriptive information. *Here* and *there* are pure deictics. Impure deictics convey additional descriptive information. For instance, *he* not only locates the referent relative to the speech event (i.e. is neither speaker nor addressee), but also indicates that the referent is singular and male.

Q

qualia roles   The notion of qualia roles was introduced by Pustejovsky. It will be illustrated as it applies to nouns. The idea is that the properties of concepts can be divided into a small number of types, and that different types are activated in different contexts. This has an effect on the interpretation of a noun in different contexts. Pustejovsky proposes four qualia roles: formal, constitutive, telic, and agentive:

formal: This includes information about an item's position in a **taxonomy**, what it is a type of, and what sub-types it includes.

constitutive: This includes information about an item's part-whole structure, its physical attributes like size, weight, and what it is made of, and sensory attributes like colour and smell.

telic: This includes information about how an item characteristically interacts with other entities, whether as agent or instrument, in purposeful activities.

agentive: This includes information about an item's 'life-history', how it came into being, and how it will end its existence.

A specification of the meaning of a noun will contain information under each of these headings. Part of the evidence that these divisions are real is that they can give rise to sharp distinctions in interpretation that are reminiscent of ambiguity. For instance, the verb *finish* requires the specification of an action to complete it. Very often this action does not need to be explicitly stated as it can be recovered from the appropriate qualia role. However, if two different qualia roles indicate different possible actions, then a sentence can appear ambiguous. Take, for instance, *Pete finished the book yesterday*. This can mean (at least) two different things, either (a) that he finished reading the book (the telic role for *book* will specify that a book is for reading) or (b) that he finished writing the book (the agentive role will indicate that a book characteristically comes into being by being written).

quantifiers   For linguists, a quantifier is an expression like *some*, *a few*, *many*, *several*, *a lot of*, and so on, which indicates a quantity of something (usually numerals are excluded). In the **predicate calculus** there are two quantifiers, the universal operator and the existential operator.

quasi-hyponymy   see **sense relations**

R

ratified participant   see under **speech event participant**

reading   A specific interpretation of a word in a specific context. For instance, *CD* has a different reading in *a beautiful CD* and *an unbreakable CD*; *sad* has a different reading in *a sad story* and *a sad person*.

reference   see **definite reference, indefinite reference, generic reference**

reflexive pronoun   The reflexive pronouns in English end in *-self* (*myself*, *yourself*, *herself*, etc.). They have several meanings. One meaning is self-directed action, as in *Pete killed himself*. Another emphasises that no other agent is involved, as in *She did it herself*. Yet another sense adds a kind of emphasis: *The prime minister himself did not know of the plan.* Other uses of reflexive pronouns can be found in other languages. To give one example, in French, a reflexive can signal a **middle voice**: *La porte s'ouvrit* ('The door opened').

reflexive (relation)   A reflexive relation is one which holds between an entity and itself, such as 'is identical in appearance to', 'has the same name as', and so on. (There is a normal presumption that in, for instance, *X has the same name as Y*, X and Y are not the same. However, it is arguable that this is not a logical fact, but an **implicature**.)

regular (systematic) polysemy   Many cases of polysemy are systematic in the sense that the same relation between polysemous senses can be observed over a range of words. As a result, the appearance of polysemy can be at least partly predicted on the basis of meaning. Many cases involve **metonymy**. An example is the use of words whose primary referents are types of fruit or flower to refer to the plants/trees themselves or their seeds, bulbs, and so on:

We picked some apples/pears/plums/tomatoes/raspberries.
We planted some apples/pears/plums/tomatoes/raspberries.
We picked some marigolds/sweet peas/pansies/dahlias.
We sowed some marigolds/sweet peas/pansies/dahlias.

Many verbal nouns show an alternation between 'fact' and 'manner' readings:

Pete's leaving was unexpected ('the fact that he left').
Pete's leaving was chaotic ('his manner of leaving').

relative (syncategorematic) adjectives Adjectives that denote degrees of a variable property like length, weight, speed, or temperature. They are known as 'relative' because the absolute value of the property they denote depends on the entity they describe. For instance, *a fast walker* cannot go as fast as *a fast car*, nor does *a heavy suitcase* weigh as much as *a heavy lorry*. Relative adjectives are interpreted as implicit comparatives, that is to say, they indicate a value that is greater than some implicit reference value for the property in question. It is sometimes suggested that the appropriate reference value is an average value for the category denoted by the noun, so that, for instance, *a large mouse* indicates a mouse that is larger than the average mouse. However, while this may be the default interpretation, in actual use reference points can be heavily dependent on context. Consider, for instance, the height of the desired individual when a teacher says to the class: *I want somebody tall to help me clear these shelves*. Obviously, the meaning of *tall* here depends on the age of the children in the class (compare **absolute adjectives**).

Relevance Theory This is a theory of **implicature** which incorporates some aspects of Grice's approach (see under **Co-operative Principle, conventional implicature, conversational implicature, maxims of conversation**), but takes it in a new direction. As in Grice's theory, the notion of (conversational) implicature is central. Relevance theorists, however, regard Grice's maxims as arbitrary in number and deficient in explanatory power. They argue that one of Grice's maxims, the Maxim of Relation ('Be relevant'), when appropriately developed, can do the work of all the others, and they accordingly raise it to the status of an overall principle to supplant Grice's Co-operative Principle. This principle, called the 'principle of relevance', has two parts, the 'cognitive principle of relevance' and the 'communicative principle of relevance'. According to the cognitive principle of relevance, the human cognitive system interprets an utterance in such a way as to maximise its relevance. This means achieving the greatest number of 'contextual effects' (changes in the information stored in the cognitive system) while minimising the cost in terms of processing effort. According to the communicative principle of relevance, a bona fide communicator, simply by producing an utterance, implicates his or her belief that it is optimally relevant. The speaker is the more active participant in two-way communication; the hearer is more passive. The speaker's task is to produce an utterance which will enable the hearer to construe the intended message by following the standard procedure. To do this, the speaker must take account of the hearer's knowledge and of how accessible its different parts are. The standard procedure for the hearer is to test possible interpretations in order of processing effort required, beginning with the most accessible, until one is found whose contextual effects justify the processing effort expended. If the speaker has done his or her job properly, the first such interpretation will be the correct one. Two phases of interpreting an utterance can be distinguished. The first is the extraction of the 'explicature'. The explicature is basically what is explicitly encoded in the linguistic form of the utterance, together with certain elaborations that are needed to make it logically complete and unambiguous. Consider, for instance, B's reply in the following:

A: When did you arrive?
B: Yesterday.

In order to function as explicature this needs at least

two sorts of elaboration. First, it must be expanded to *I arrived yesterday*. Second, *yesterday* designates a particular day, and this must be specified in absolute terms (not just as 'the day before the day including the time of utterance'). The second phase is the combination of explicature with context to produce **implicatures**.

repair   see under **conversational analysis**

reversives   see under **directional opposites**

rigid designator   see under **possible world semantics**

$\boxed{S}$

salience (prominence)   Something in a perceptual field is salient to the extent that it readily becomes the focus of attention. This may be because it actively attracts attention more than its neighbours or surroundings, or because it requires less cognitive effort to bring it to the centre of attention. Linguistic expressions make certain parts of a domain salient by profiling. Of two profiled elements, one may be more salient than the other (see **trajector and landmark**). Mere mention may enhance salience, hence, the maleness of a father is rendered more salient by describing him as a *male parent* than by describing him as a *father*.

scalar implicatures   see under **generalised vs particularised conversational implicatures**

scanning (summary and sequential)   The two types of scanning are **construal** operations, claimed by Langacker to be important in distinguishing verbal meanings (in general) from nominal and adjectival meanings. The use of a finite verb induces a sequential construal, which conceptualises an event as a dynamic unrolling through time: *The building collapsed.* Changing a verb into a noun changes the construal to a summary one, presenting the event as a static conception: *The collapse of the building.* Nouns like *chair* and *water*, and adjectives like *red* and *afraid* are also claimed to embody summary scanning. The dynamic nature of sequential scanning does not require ongoing change: the distinction between sequential and summary scanning can be clearly felt with stative verbs: Pete resembles his father, *Pete's resemblance to his father.*

scope   This refers to the range of applicability of an item in a linguistic expression with respect to other items in the same expression. Often there is a choice of range, giving rise to scope ambiguity. Take the classic case of *old men and women*: we do not know, out of context, whether *old* applies only to *men* or to *men and women*. Another case concerns the relation between **presuppositions** and negation. A sentence like *Pete has not stopped smoking* has two interpretations, depending on whether the presupposition that Pete was a smoker falls within the scope of the negative or not. If the presupposition is outside the scope of the negative, then the meaning is that Pete still smokes. This is the default reading of the sentence. However, the sentence can also be used to deny the presupposition as well as the stopping: *Pete has NOT stopped smoking – he never HAS smoked.* As a final example of scope variation, consider the sentence *All the dogs chased a rabbit.* This has two interpretations, according to whether (1) all the dogs chased the same rabbit or (2) each dog chased a rabbit, but not necessarily the same one. This distinction can be captured using the universal quantifier and the existential quantifier in **predicate logic**:

1. $\forall x \: [\text{dog }(x) \Rightarrow \exists y \: [\text{rabbit }(y) \: \& \: \text{chase }(x)(y)]]$
   ("For every x, if x was a dog, then there was a y such that y was a rabbit and x chased y")
2. $\exists y \: [\text{rabbit }(y) \: \& \: \forall x \: [\text{dog }(x) \Rightarrow \text{chase }(x)(y)]]$
   ("There exists some y such that y is a rabbit and for all x such that x is a dog, x chased y")

In (1) the universal quantifier is said to have 'wider scope' and the existential quantifier 'narrower scope'; in (2) the relations are reversed.

scripts   These are related to **frames**. The term is usually applied to stereotyped sequences of actions that constitute a global event, such as a visit to a restaurant or a dentist, a race, a birthday party, and so on.

secondary tense   see under **temporal deixis**

selectional restrictions   We do not have complete freedom in combining words together in utterances: virtually all words combine normally with some words and less normally with others. Indeed, this is a condition of their having meaning. For instance, the verb *pour* forms a normal combination with *wine* as a direct object (*Pete poured the wine*), but not with *glasses* (*?Pete poured the glasses*). The conditions for normal combination are commonly called *selectional restrictions*. In some cases, the task of specifying selectional restrictions seems relatively straightforward. For instance, we can say that for the combination *a pregnant X* to be normal (at least on a literal reading), X must possess the features [MATURE] [FEMALE] [ANIMAL], or at least must not possess features belonging to the same set of mutually **incompatible** features as any of these. This predicts that *a pregnant* *cow* and *my pregnant neighbour* are normal, and that *pregnant baby*, *pregnant postman*, and *pregnant lamp-post* are all odd because of feature incompatibility. In other cases, specifying the restrictions is not so easy. Take the case of *pour*, cited above. It might seem that *pour* simply requires that its direct object refer to a liquid. However, one can also pour salt, sugar, rice and so on. Perhaps it requires something that is capable of *flowing*? This is not sufficient either, because air can flow and electricity flows along wires, but neither of these can be poured. There is no easy answer. One approach is to say that the direct object of *pour* is prototypically a liquid, but that there is no clear boundary between acceptable and unacceptable objects. (Those who take this view are more likely to speak of 'selectional preferences'.) Selectional restrictions typically operate in a specific direction, in the sense that, given a sequence XY, starting from one of the elements it is possible to see that normal partners must fall within a particular semantic domain, whereas starting from the other element no such generalisation is possible. Take the case of *pour wine*. Starting from *pour*, we can at least intuit a resemblance among all the possibilities for a normal sequence. This is not possible, however, if we start from *wine*. Think of all the things one can do with wine: *drink*, *buy*, *lay down*, *taste*, *avoid*, *waste*, *decant*, *fortify*, and so on. These do not fall into any statable semantic domain. The selectional restrictions thus operate from *pour* to the direct object noun-phrase, rather than in the opposite direction. Generally speaking, modifiers select their heads, but heads select their complements (for an explanation of these terms, see under **semantic heads**).

semantic change   The meanings of words have a tendency to change over time. There are various ways of describing the types of change which occur. The following list covers the principal ones.

1. Gain and loss (of meaning): With the advent of personal computers, an obvious example of a word that has gained a meaning is *mouse*. A word which has lost a meaning is *direction*. In Jane Austen's day, one of the meanings of *direction* was what we now call *address* (e.g. on an envelope). This represents a concomitant gain for the word *address*. A new meaning is frequently a **metaphoric** or **metonymic** extension from an earlier meaning.

2. Change of **default** meaning: A primary meaning may become secondary, or vice versa. A hundred years ago the primary meaning of *expire* was 'die'. This meaning still exists but it is somewhat archaic. The primary meaning now is 'come to the end of a period of validity'. Another example is the change in the dominant meaning of *intercourse* from non-sexual to sexual activity.

3. Semantic drift: As the details of everyday life change gradually, there is often a gradual shift in the meanings of words. One such shift is a change in the prototype of a category. Think of the gradual change in the prototype of a *weapon* or *vehicle* over the centuries.

4. Specialisation and generalisation: These terms refer to the widening or narrowing of category boundaries. Specialisation is illustrated by *doctor*, which at one time meant simply 'teacher' or 'learned person'. An example of generalisation is *actor*, which originally denoted only male thespians, but is now used without discrimination of gender.

5. Pejoration and amelioration: Words which originally expressed a positive or neutral attitude some-

times come to be derogatory, or at least express a negative judgement. One example of this is *interfere*, which originally meant simply 'intervene', without the negative overtones it now has. Another example is *typical* in *Isn't that just typical?* Historically, words referring to women have been particularly prone to pejoration: *mistress*, *madam*, *working girl*. Change in the opposite direction, known as amelioration, is somewhat rarer; perhaps the development of *queen* from an earlier form meaning simply 'woman' or 'wife' is an example, although this word has also undergone pejoration at various times. Another example is *sturdy*, which had a pejorative meaning of 'reckless, violent, obstinate', but now has a positive meaning.

6. Bleaching: This refers to a loss of meaning, as with, for example, *make* in *to make a phone call*, where the original meaning of 'construct' has virtually disappeared, leaving only something like 'do something'. The term also applies to a weakening of meaning, as with words such as *awful*, *terrible*, *fantastic*.

semantic components (also semantic features, semantic primes)   Supposed indivisible atoms of meaning which combine to form more complex meanings. An example of a complex meaning analysable into more basic semantic atoms is 'girl', which is built up out of the components [YOUNG] + [FEMALE] + [HUMAN]. Each of these components also participates in the meanings of other words:

'boy' = [YOUNG] + [MALE] + [HUMAN]
'man' = [ADULT] + [MALE] + [HUMAN]
'filly' = [YOUNG] + [FEMALE] + [HORSE]

Semantic components provide one way of formalising **sense relations**. Take the case of **hyponymy** as it relates to the words *animal*, *horse*, and *mare*. Suppose the meaning of *animal* is expressed as [ANIMAL], the meaning of *horse* as [EQUINE][ANIMAL], and that of *mare* as [FEMALE][EQUINE][ANIMAL] (or some equivalent decomposition). We can then give a general rule that a word W^1 is a hyponym of a second word W^2 if and only if all the components which define W^2 are included in the components defining W^1. Hence, if we define *filly* as [ANIMAL][EQUINE][FEMALE][YOUNG], then *filly* will be a hyponym of not only *mare*, but also of *horse* and *animal*. On this approach, an account of the structural relations within the vocabulary of a language requires a componential analysis of every word, together with a set of rules like the one just illustrated. A distinction is sometimes made between semantic components and semantic features, whereby a feature is a component which has been assigned a value of '+' or '−' (positive or negative). In this system, the notions 'male' and 'female' might be assigned to the same component, with 'male' being represented by means of the feature [+MALE] and 'female' by [−MALE]. The exact nature of semantic components, and their significance, depends heavily on the theory of which they form part. Typically, however, they are held to be restricted in number (far fewer than the number of possible word-meanings, for example), but able to combine in various ways to form a much larger number of complex meanings. The components do this in much the same way as a limited inventory of phonemes gives rise to a much larger number of word forms. They are also usually considered to be universal in the sense that they can be observed in all human languages; they are often claimed to be an inherent feature of the human conceptual system (see also binarism, structural semantics, Natural Semantic Metalanguage).

semantic field   This term is sometimes used as an equivalent to **lexical field**. It can also be used to refer to a conceptual area, independently of how it is divided up lexically.

semantic heads   The semantic head of a construction is the part of the construction which determines the **selectional restrictions** (or preferences) of the whole construction. Take the sentence *The old tree jumped over the stream*, which most people will agree is anomalous. Can we locate the semantic clash? Perhaps it is between *old* and *jumped*? If so, we should be able to 'cure' the anomaly by substituting another adjective for *old*. However, this does not seem to be possible: *young*, *tall*, *shady*, and *sturdy* are all just as bad. Changing *tree*, on the other hand, can normalise the sentence: *The old man jumped over the stream*. This allows us to conclude that *tree* is one of the parties to the clash; a similar chain of reasoning will lead us to the conclusion that the other culprit is *jumped* (rather than *over the stream*). Hence *tree* is the semantic head of the construction *the old tree*, and *jumped* is the head of *jumped over the stream*. Constructions can be divided into 'head-modifier' constructions and 'head-complement' constructions. A full account of this distinction is not possible here, but, briefly, a modifier is always optional in the sense that it can always be omitted without making the construction ungrammatical. Typical head-modifier constructions are: adjective-noun (*ripe apples*), verb-adverb (*walk quickly*), and adverb-adjective (*very hot*). In the case of a head-complement construction, by contrast, there are always at least some instances where the complement cannot be omitted, or if it can, then the element is **latent**.

Typical head-complement constructions are: verb-object (*stroked the cat*) and preposition-object (*on the table*). The distinction between modifiers and complements has consequences for the direction of selectional preferences: modifiers select their heads, but heads select their modifiers (for the directionality of selection see under **selectional restrictions**).

semantic opacity   see under **compositionality**

semes and classemes   These are types of **semantic components** distinguished in certain versions of **structural semantics**. Semes are semantic units which serve to distinguish members of a particular **lexical field** from one another, but which have no currency outside the field. In the field of animals, for instance, the sense units which distinguish *cat*, *dog*, *horse*, and so on from one another ([FELINE], [CANINE], [EQUINE]) are semes. Classemes are sense units with very general meanings which participate in more than one field and which are frequently expressed grammatically. Examples are [ANIMATE], [INANIMATE], [MALE], [FEMALE].

semiotics   The general study of **signs** (which includes, but is not exhausted by, linguistic signs).

sense   The use of this word in linguistics is not consistent, and can be confusing. The following are the main uses.

1. According to one influential view, the sense of, say, a word, is constituted by its meaning relations with other words in the same language, rather than by its relation to things in the world. So, for instance, the sense of *dog* consists of a set of meaning relations, including the facts that it is a **hyponym** of

animal, it has hyponyms such as *collie* and *spaniel*, it is an **incompatible** of *cat*, *cow*, *camel*, and so on, and it **collocates** with words like *bark* and *growl*.

2. The term *sense* is often used with a meaning equivalent to **intension**.

3. We can say of a polysemous or homonymous word that it 'has several senses'. Here, the word refers to distinguishable meanings, as they might appear in a dictionary, but is uncommitted as between (1) and (2) above. For a word to be described as having more than one sense, it must satisfy the criteria for **ambiguity**.

senses (lexical)   see **lexical senses**

sense relations (lexical relations)   There are two main ways of looking at sense relations. According to the viewpoint of **structural semantics**, the **sense** of a word is the sum total of its sense relations with other words in the language. Outside of structural semantics, sense relations are usually regarded as relations between senses (or other units of meaning). Sense relations are of two main types, 'paradigmatic' and 'syntagmatic'. Paradigmatic relations hold between items which can occupy the same position in a grammatical structure: *I saw a bird/sparrow* (**hyponymy**); *I saw a crow/sparrow* (**incompatibility**); *a long/short journey* (**antonymy**); *She touched Pete's arm/elbow* (**meronymy**). Ideally, words that stand in paradigmatic relations should be of the same grammatical category, but sometimes they are not. For instance, there is no **hyperonym** of which the following adjectives are hyponyms: *round*, *square*, *oval*, *oblong*, and *triangular*. However, they are all related in a hyponym-like way to the noun *shape*. Relations of this type are sometimes called 'quasi-relations'; the commonest of these is quasi-hyponymy. For more detail on individual relations, see under **antonyms** (1 and 2), **complementaries, converses, directional opposites, hyponyms, incompatibles, meronyms, reversives, taxonyms**. Syntagmatic sense relations hold between items in the same grammatical structure. Relations between individual items are not usually given names on the lines of hyponymy, antonymy, and so forth, but certain effects of putting meanings together are recognised, such as **anomaly** (e.g. *a light green illness*) and **pleonasm** (e.g. *dental toothache*). The requirements for a 'normal' combination are described as **selectional restrictions** or selectional preferences.

sentence meaning vs utterance meaning   Sentence meaning is the meaning a sentence has by virtue of the words it contains and their grammatical arrangement, and which is not dependent on context. Utterance meaning is the meaning a sentence carries when it is used in a particular context, with referents assigned to all referring expressions, and taking into account any **conversational implicatures**.

sequential scanning   see under **scanning (summary and sequential)**

signs   Entities that stand for other entities in communication. They may be visual, auditory, olfactory, tactile, and so on. They may be established or spontaneous. They may form part of a complex system: a language is an organised system of signs. For some important subdivisions of signs, see under **arbitrary vs iconic signs, natural vs conventional signs, discrete vs continuous signs, paralinguistic signs**.

simile   A simile involves an explicit comparison between two things or actions. The majority of similes include the word *like*: *You are behaving like a spoilt child*, *Their house is like a renaissance palace*. *As if* is also quite frequent: *He treats her as if she were a delicate piece of porcelain*. Normally the relevant features of resemblance signalled by a simile are quite circumscribed, and its wording frequently serves to narrow down the possibilities. That is to say, similes like *Pete is like a lion*, with no indication as to what the relevant resemblances are between Pete and a lion, are relatively rare. A more typical simile is *Her teeth flashed like steel under the neon lights*. If we were simply told that 'her' teeth 'were like steel', we might well wonder what interpretation to adopt; knowing that the relevant feature is the way light is reflected makes interpretation easier. Not all expressions of the form *X is like Y* are accepted as similes by most semanticists. For instance, *Your kitchen is very like mine* would not be considered to be a simile by many. True similes are considered by many to be a type of **figurative** language. A rough-and-ready way of distinguishing 'true similes' from 'literal similes' is to see what happens when they are transformed into metaphors: a literal simile will either not make sense at all or will suffer a major change in meaning, whereas a true simile yields a metaphor whose meaning is close to that of the simile: *Peter is like a lion* (true simile) vs *Peter is a lion* (metaphor); *Your kitchen is like mine* (literal simile) vs *?Your kitchen is mine* (metaphor not possible).

singular   A term in the **number system** of a language that denotes one of whatever is being counted. Strictly, we do not speak of a singular unless the language has a number system with at least one other option (normally **plural**, if there is only one).

social deixis   Social deictics are expressions whose function is to indicate the position of the referent on the scales of social status and intimacy relative to the speaker. A prototypical example is the use of the so-called T/V pronouns. For more details, see under **politeness**.

sortal crossing   see **zeugma**

sortal predicate   A predicate which indicates the sort or kind a particular entity belongs to. For instance, *gift* is not a sortal predicate, because gifts belong to many different kinds, but *necklace* is. A sortal category is one whose members belong by virtue of being of a specific kind.

source domain   see under **Conceptual Metaphor Theory**

spatial deixis   Spatial deictics indicate location in space relative to the speaker. The most basic spatial deictics are the adverbs *here* and *there*. These can be glossed 'place near to the speaker' and 'place not near to the speaker'. Modern English has only two terms, but older forms of English and some dialects have a third term *yonder*, *yon*, which indicates a greater distance than *there* and can be glossed 'far from the speaker'. Notice that the boundary between *here* and *there* is heavily context-bound: *here in this room*, *here in Manchester*, *here in Britain*, *here on earth*, and so on. The demonstratives *this* and *that* are usually considered to be spatial deictics in their basic use, although they often have a more abstract meaning. For instance, *this theory* and *that theory* do not locate the theory in literal space, but do indicate a more abstract closeness and distance from the speaker. *This* and *here* are called proximal deictics, and *that* and *there* distal deictics. Some scholars emphasise correspondences between proximal deictics and first person deictics, and between distal and second and third person deictics. Spatial deictics can indicate psychological, rather than strictly spatial distance: *This is great news*, *That theory is rubbish*, *I can't stand that man*.

specialisation   see **semantic change**

specificity   This is the property which distinguishes a **hyponym** from a **hyperonym**: the hyponym is more specific, the hyperonym more general. The hyponym gives more detailed information and denotes a narrower category. Thus, *dog* is more specific than *animal*, *scarlet* than *red*, and *sprint* than *run*. The converse of specificity is generality (sometimes called schematicity). A different type of specificity holds between a **meronym** and a **holonym**: *finger*, for instance, is more specific than *hand*.

speech acts   These are acts which crucially involve the production of language. It is usual to recognise three basic types: locutionary acts, illocutionary acts and perlocutionary acts.

1. Locutionary act: the production of an utterance, with a particular intended structure, meaning, and reference. (These provisos are meant to rule out the mindless production of language such as by parrots and computers.)
2. Illocutionary act: an act performed by a speaker in saying something (with an appropriate intention and in an appropriate context), rather than by virtue of having produced a particular effect by saying something. For instance, if someone says *I order you to leave now* they have performed the act of ordering, simply by virtue of having uttered

the words, whether or not the addressee acts in the desired way.

3. Perlocutionary act: a speech act which depends on the production of a specific effect. For instance, for the verbal act of persuasion to have occurred, in *Pete persuaded Liz to marry him*, it is not enough for Pete to have uttered certain words – what is essential is that a previously reluctant addressee is caused to act in an appropriate way.

Every illocutionary act has a particular 'illocutionary force'. This may be explicitly signalled by the use of a **performative verb** such as *beg*, *promise*, *command*, *suggest*, *congratulate*, or *thank*, or a particular grammatical form, as in *Go away!*, *Have you seen Pete?*, or it may be implicit, in which case it must be inferred, largely on the basis of contextual evidence. For instance, an utterance such as *You will never see me again* may function, in different circumstances, as a threat, a promise, a simple statement of fact, or a prediction. For a particular illocutionary act to function normally, it is typically the case that certain contextual conditions need to be satisfied. These conditions are known as **felicity conditions**. There are various ways of classifying illocutionary acts. The following is an example:

Assertives: these commit the speaker to the truth of what is said: *assert*, *aver*, *boast*, *claim*, *report*.

Directives: these are aimed at getting someone to act in a certain way: *beg*, *implore*, *request*, *warn (to)*, *recommend (to)*, *ask (to)*.

Commissives: these have the effect of committing the speaker to some action in the future: *promise*, *undertake*, *offer*, *threaten*.

Expressives: these express the speaker's feelings or attitude: *thank*, *congratulate*, *forgive*.

Declaratives: these are said to produce a change of some sort in the world: *resign*, *sack*, *appoint*, *name*, *christen*, *sentence (in court)*, *bid (at auction)*.

speech event participants   The following may be recognised:

Speaker: the person producing an utterance.

Addressee: the person to whom an utterance is directed in a speech event.

Ratified participant: a member of a conversational group not directly addressed, who is expected to attend to what is said.

Overhearer: this may be a 'bystander' (who may understand and join in conversation without causing offence) or an 'eavesdropper' (who is not supposed to hear).

standard (conversational) implicatures   These are conversational implicatures which can be inferred from an utterance, provided we assume that the speaker is following the **maxims of conversation** as far as possible. Consider this scenario:

A: Can I speak to Jane?
B: She's in the shower.

A will deduce from B's answer that this is an inconvenient time to speak to Jane, although B does not explicitly say so. What justifies A's inference? Part of the answer is that B will assume that A is obeying the Maxim of Relation, and that the answer is therefore relevant. The most obvious relevance is that calling Jane to the phone would cause inconvenience. Or take the following example:

A: Did Pete post the letter and pay the newspaper bill?

B: He posted the letter.

B's answer implicates either that Pete did not pay the newspaper bill, or that B does not know whether he did or not (more context would be needed to choose between these). Why? B appears not to be following the Maxim of Quantity, in that the utterance does not provide the required amount of information. However, assuming that B is nonetheless obeying the **Co-operative Principle**, we can infer that there is good reason for the poverty of information. One possibility is adherence to the Maxim of Quality: B is giving as much information as he or she has evidence for. A might therefore infer that B does not know whether or not Pete paid the paper bill. (Contrast with **flouting the (conversational) maxims**.)

strength of implicatures   Implicatures can vary in strength according to the degree of the speaker's commitment to them, how easily the speaker could deny intending them, and how easily the hearer can avoid drawing them. For instance, B's answer in (1) carries a strong implicature that he or she has exactly four children:

  1. A: How many children do you have?
      B: Four.

However, the implicature of exactitude is much weaker in (2):

  2. A: You need to have four children to qualify for this allowance.
      B: I have four children.

And in (3), the implicature of exactness ('four minutes and no less than four minutes') is probably absent altogether:

  3. A: You have to be able to do the 1500 metres in

four minutes to enter.
B: I can do it in four minutes.

In (4), B's reply carries a number of weakish implicatures involving sexist and ageist prejudices that he could probably deny if challenged:

4. A: Who was driving?
    B: Some old woman. (Compare *An old lady*.)

structural semantics A branch of structural linguistics, which derives from the work of the Swiss scholar Saussure. His original ideas were further developed by later scholars and this resulted in different versions of structural semantics. The fundamental idea underlying structural semantics is that word meanings are basically relational; that is to say, a word's meaning is determined by its position in a network of semantic relations with other words in the same lexical field. Both **paradigmatic** and **syntagmatic** relations are relevant here (although some structural semanticists have emphasised one of these and some have emphasised the other). A 'lexical field' is a coherent subset of the vocabulary whose members are interlinked by paradigmatic and syntagmatic relations of **sense**. This approach to word meaning is sometimes referred to as **lexical field** theory. We may take *dog* as a concrete example. The meaning of *dog* is determined partly by its paradigmatic relations. For instance, it has *cat*, *mouse*, *camel*, and *rhinoceros* as **incompatibles**, *spaniel*, *Pekinese*, and *collie* as **hyponyms**, *tail*, *paw*, and *dewlap* as **meronyms**, and is itself a hyponym of *mammal*, *animal*, *living thing* and so on. (Fields can be nested within more inclusive fields.) Also relevant are its syntagmatic relations with words like *bark*, *whine*, and *growl*, to mention but a few. Or take the word *auburn*. An important part of the meaning of this word is its syntagmatic relation with *hair*. But its paradigmatic relations are equally important: it is a member of a set of incompatible co-hyponyms including *ginger*, *black*, *white*, *brown*, *blonde*, and *grey*.

A lexical field divides up a conceptual field among its members. According to the strictest version of field theory, the conceptual field is exhaustively partitioned among the members of the lexical field, that is to say, there are no gaps; furthermore, the semantic value of any word is circumscribed by those of other words in the field. This has three important consequences. First, a word in a particular language that participates in a number of different lexical fields will have a different semantic value in each of them. Take the word *red* in English (in its 'colour' sense). This participates in at least three different lexical fields: a default field in which it contrasts with *orange*, *yellow*, *green*, *blue*, *purple*, *brown*, *black*, *white*, and *grey*; a field denoting types of wine, in which it contrasts with *white*, and *rosé*; and a field denoting hair colours, in which it contrasts with *black*, *white*, *brown*, *blonde*, *fair*, and *grey*. In the default field, the range of colours denoted by *red* is limited by the ranges of *purple*, *orange*, and *brown*. In the 'wine' field, *red* has only two contrasts, *white* and *rosé*. As a result, it covers a different range of colours, including, for instance, hues that in the default field would be labelled *purple* in the case of *red wine*, and *green* and *yellow* in the case of *white wine*. A second consequence arises from the fact that different languages may partition a particular conceptual field in different ways, and make a different number of distinctions; hence, there may be no translational equivalence between terms, or terms which may superficially appear to be equivalents actually have different values. For instance, the conceptual field covered by the English words *hamlet*, *village*, *town*, and *city* is partitioned in French by *hameau*, *village*, *bourg*, and *ville*. However, with the possible exception of *hamlet* and *hameau*, there are no exact correspondences between the two languages. The English distinction between *town* and *city* is not lexically marked in French, while the French distinction between *village* and *bourg* is not made in English. (A *bourg* is a largish village, typically the main village in a commune, with a *mairie* (mayor's office) and a church. Most examples of *bourg* would be called villages by English speakers.) The third consequence is that a change in the part of a conceptual field covered by a word entails a change in the ranges of other words in the same field. An extension in the range of *red* in the direction of *orange* would cause a corresponding reduction in the range of *orange* and/or *purple*. A related consequence is that it is not possible to have a full grasp of one member of a field without also knowing the other members. One does not know fully what *horse* means unless one has a grasp of the types of 'non-horse'. A structuralist approach to semantics may take a **componential** or a **non-componential** direction (based, for instance, on **meaning postulates**). However, in both cases an analysis must be justified in terms of the structural relations within a given vocabulary.

subjunctive mood   see under **mood**

sub terms   see under **polar antonyms**

subordinate (level of categorisation)   Conceptual categories at the subordinate level are sub-divisions of **basic-level categories**. For instance, the category DOG is subdivided into the subordinate-level categories SPANIEL, COLLIE, ALSATIAN, POODLE, PEKINESE, and so on. Some of these are further sub-divided. Members of categories at this level show a high degree of mutual resemblance, but the features which differentiate the members of one category from those of sister categories are fewer than for basic level categories. The names of subordinate-level categories are often morphologically or lexically complex:

Basic-level	Subordinate-level
spoon	*teaspoon, coffee spoon, soup spoon*
cat	*tabby cat, Manx cat, Persian cat*
saw	*fretsaw, tenon-saw, rip saw, hacksaw*
rose	*rambler rose, hybrid tea rose*

summary scanning   see under **scanning (summary and sequential)**

superlative   see under **degrees of comparison**

superordinate (1)   see under **hyponymy**

superordinate (2) (level of categorisation)   Conceptual categories at the superordinate level are more inclusive than **basic-level categories**. For instance, the superordinate category ANIMAL includes such basic-level categories as CAT, DOG, WOLF, ELEPHANT, CROCODILE, and so on. Members of categories at this level are well differentiated from members of other categories, but they have a lower degree of mutual resemblance than those of basic-level categories. The names of superordinate-level categories are often **mass nouns,** although the names of their constituent basic-level categories are **count nouns:**

Basic-level	Superordinate-level
knives, spoons, forks	*cutlery*
chairs, tables, beds	*furniture*
cups, plates, saucers	*crockery*
vests, bras, knickers	*underwear*

(Sometimes the relationship is the other way round:)

salt, pepper, vinegar	*condiments*
copper, gold, zinc	*metals*

supra terms   see under **polar antonyms**

syllepsis   see **zeugma**

symbolic deixis   This refers to the use of a **deictic** expression where close monitoring of the situation by the hearer is not required because the relations between the speaker and the things referred to are relatively stable and do not change over the course of a conversation or discourse: *I've lived here all my life, Nobody cares these days, Those bastards are just out to get you.*

symmetry (of a relation)   see under **logical relations**

Sympathy Maxim   One of the Maxims of Politeness proposed by Leech:

Maximise sympathy (expression of positive feelings) towards hearer.

Minimise antipathy (expression of negative feelings) towards hearer.

On the basis of this principle, congratulations, condolences, and commiserations are inherently polite. If negative feelings must be expressed, they should be played down. In the following examples someone has had an accident, due to carelessness:

Serves you right! (not polite)
You really need to be more careful (more polite)
These things happen (even more polite)

syncategorematic adjectives   see **relative adjectives**

synonymy, synonyms   A word is said to be a synonym of another word in the same language if one or more of its senses bears a sufficiently close similarity to one or more of the senses of the other word. It should be noted that complete identity of meaning (absolute synonymy) is very rarely, if ever, encountered. Words would be absolute synonyms if there were no contexts in which substituting one for the other had any semantic effect. However, given that a basic function of words is to be semantically distinctive, it is not surprising that such identical pairs are rare. That being so, the problem of characterising synonymy is one of specifying what kind and degree of semantic difference is permitted. One possibility is to define synonymy as 'propositional synonymy': two words A and B are synonyms if substituting either one for the other in an utterance has no effect on the **propositional meaning** (i.e. **truth conditions**) of the utterance. This is the case with, for instance, *begin: commence* and *false: untrue* (on the relevant readings):

> The concert began/commenced with Beethoven's Egmont Overture.
> What he told me was false/untrue.

By this definition, synonyms will typically differ in respect of **non-propositional** aspects of meaning, such as expressive meaning and evoked meaning. Thus, *begin* and *commence* differ in register; the difference between *false* and *untrue* (indicating lack of veracity) is rather subtle, but the former is more condemnatory, perhaps because of a stronger presumption of deliberateness. However, while this is a convenient and easily applied way of defining synonymy, it does not capture the way the notion is used by, for instance, lexicographers, in the compilation of dictionaries of synonyms or in the assembly of groups of words for information on 'synonym discrimination'. Certainly, some of the words in such lists are propositional synonyms, but others are not, and for these we need some such notion as 'near-synonymy' ('plesionymy'). This is not easy to define, but roughly speaking, near-synonyms must share the same core meaning and must not have the primary function of contrasting with one another in their most typical contexts. (For instance, *collie* and *spaniel* share much of their meaning, but they contrast in their most typical contexts.) Examples of near-synonyms are: *murder: execute: assassinate*; *withhold: detain*; *joyful: cheerful*; *heighten: enhance*; *injure: damage*; *idle: inert: passive*.

syntagmatic sense relations   see under **sense relations**

synthetic proposition   A proposition whose truth value is determined by the relation between its meaning and the way the world is, not by its meaning alone: 'Tony Blair likes guava jelly for breakfast.' (Compare **analytic proposition**.)

$\boxed{\text{T}}$

Tact and Generosity Maxims   These are members of the set of Maxims of Politeness proposed by Leech. They form a natural pair, the former being oriented towards the hearer, and the latter towards the speaker. The following is a slight modification of Leech's formulation:

Tact Maxim: Minimise cost to the hearer.
                   Maximise benefit to the hearer.

Generosity Maxim: Minimise benefit to self.
                   Maximise cost to self.

Both of these maxims apply particularly to **speech acts** which are directives or commissives. Both of them relate to the idea of a 'cost-benefit scale'. Actions (requested or offered) can be ranked according to the cost or benefit (physical, psychological, financial, or whatever) to the person carrying them out. For instance, digging the garden probably represents a greater (physical) cost than mowing the lawn, which in turn is greater than picking some flowers; on the positive side, taking a week's holiday is a greater benefit than sitting down for a few minutes, and accepting a gift of £2000 is a greater benefit than accepting help with the washing up. The cost-benefit scale operates in conjunction with a 'scale of indirectness', which applies to the way a command, request, offer, (and so on) is formulated. In the case of directives, for instance, the most direct form is the **imperative**: *Wash the dishes*. Progressively more indirect are: *I want you to wash the dishes*; *Can you wash the dishes?*; *Could you wash the dishes?*; *I wonder if you would mind washing the dishes*. The general principle for both commissives and directives is that, for politeness, anything which involves cost to the hearer or benefit to the speaker should be 'softened' by being expressed indirectly, and the greater the cost the more the indirectness required. Conversely, anything that involves benefit to the hearer or cost to the speaker should be expressed directly. Hence *Could you wash the dishes?* and *I'll do the dishes* are more polite than *Wash the dishes* and *Maybe I should wash the dishes* respectively; likewise *Could I borrow your car?* and *Have another piece of* *cake* are more polite than *I'll borrow your car* and *Could you possibly have another piece of cake?*

target domain   see under **Conceptual Metaphor Theory**

taxonomy, taxonomic hierarchy   see under **lexical hierarchies**

taxonymy, taxonym   Taxonymy is a special variety of **hyponymy** that constitutes the vertical relation in a **taxonomic hierarchy** (see under **lexical hierarchy**). It is the relation expressed by *kind of* or *type of* as in *A stetson is a kind of hat*, *A pomelo is a type of citrus fruit*. Notice that not all hyponyms are taxonyms. For instance, a waitress is a woman, so *waitress* is a hyponym of *woman*, but it is odd to say *?A waitress is a kind of woman* or *?A waitress is a type of woman*. The relation of mutual exclusion between sister taxonyms (e.g. *cat*, *dog*; *apple*, *banana*) is called 'co-taxonymy', and is a variety of **incompatibility**.

telic events   see under **event-types**

telic role   see under **qualia roles**

temporal deixis   Temporal deictics indicate the timing of an event relative to the time of speaking. The only 'pure' English temporal deictics (those which give no other information) are *now*, which designates a time period overlapping with the time of speaking, and *then*, which basically means 'not now', and can point either into the future or the past: *I was much younger then*; *You'll be somewhat older by then*. Many temporal deictics give extra information, such as *tomorrow* ('the day after the day which includes the time of speaking') and *last year* ('the (calendar) year previous to the one which includes the time of speaking'). Verb tense is also deictic: *I washed the dishes, I am washing the dishes, I will wash the dishes*. It is useful, when speaking about tenses, to distinguish three points in time: the time at which the event occurred (ET), the time at which the utterance was produced (UT), and the reference time (RT). In the so-called primary tenses, past, present and future, UT and RT are the same. There are also secondary or compound tenses in which UT and RT are different. In the case of the 'pluperfect tense', RT is in the past relative to UT: *Liz had already left when I arrived* (Liz's leaving preceded my arrival, which preceded the time of speaking). In the 'future perfect tense', RT is in the future relative to UT: *By the time I arrive, Liz will have left*. It is also possible to have a 'future-in-the-past tense': *Liz was about to leave when I arrived*. Some languages have different past tense forms according to how far back in time the denoted event occurred. The most common distinction is between 'immediate past' and 'remote past', but some languages have more. Yagua (a Peruvian language) is reported to have five degrees of pastness, equivalent to 'earlier today', 'yesterday', 'within a few weeks ago', 'within a few months ago', and 'distant past'.

tenor, vehicle, and ground   These are traditional terms referring to elements of the structure of a **metaphor**. Take the metaphor *That man is a rat*. The word used metaphorically, in this case *rat*, is the vehicle. Its metaphorical meaning is the tenor (sometimes called the topic). The ground represents the resemblances or analogies which justify the metaphor.

tense   see under **temporal deixis**

thematic meaning   The two main dimensions of thematic meaning are **topic vs comment** and **given vs new information**.

thematic roles   see **functional roles**

'theory' theory   This is a theory about the nature and structure of **concepts**, one of several proposals aimed at remedying the shortcomings of the **classical theory** of concepts (see also **prototype theory, exemplar theory**). The basic idea is that a concept is represented not just by information about appearances (whatever form that might take), but more importantly by not-directly-observable properties such as causal relations, purposes, and internal constitution; in other words, a concept is like a mini theory about the members of a category. The main tenets of the 'theory' theory can be summarised as follows:

1. Conceptual representations include information about explanatory relations between features. For instance, a prototype representation of the category BIRD will include the features [CAN FLY] and [HAS WINGS], but will not include the information that wings are necessary for flight and that something like an ostrich, with insufficiently developed wings, will not be able to fly.

2. Conceptual representations give priority to properties that cannot be observed, such as the parentage and internal organs of animal species. For instance, people understand that if something starts out as, say, a cat, changing its appearance by plastic surgery until it looks exactly like a fox does not turn it into a fox, but into an unusual form of cat.

3. Humans form different types of explanatory theory

for different types of concept, such as human beings, living things, **natural kinds**, and artefacts. So, for instance, unlike the cat-fox case just described, if people are faced with, say, a screwdriver that is changed so that it looks exactly like a chisel, they are most likely to say that it has, in fact, changed into a chisel. This is because people have different sorts of theories concerning living things and artefacts.

4. Conceptual representations go through developmental stages in children which parallel developments in general human understanding and knowledge.

The 'theory' theory highlights shortcomings in both prototype theory and exemplar theory but does not rule out **prototype effects**, nor the existence of some sort of summary representation, nor the storage of information about particular examples.

token   see **type-token distinction**

topic vs comment   A topic is what some stretch of language is about. It is convenient to distinguish between the topic of an extended piece of discourse such as a paragraph, chapter, or book, and the topic of a sentence or utterance. The terms 'topic' and 'comment' usually apply to the latter: the topic is what a sentence is about and the comment is what is said about the topic. In a simple declarative sentence in English, the topic is the grammatical subject and the comment is the rest of the sentence:

1. Pete [topic] is the manager [comment].
2. Pete [topic] was sacked last week [comment].

The grammatical subject of a sentence can be regarded as the **unmarked** topic. But there are various possibilities for **marked** topics. For instance, (3) is propositionally identical to (2), but what happened to Pete is topicalised:

3. What happened to Pete last week was that he was sacked.

Notice that the topic-comment organisation of a utterance can vary independently of its given-new organisation. For instance, in (4) and (5), the topic-comment organisation remains constant, but the given-new organisation changes:

4. PETE [topic; new] is the manager [comment; given].
5. Pete [topic; given] is the MANAGER [comment; new].

In (6), the given-new structure is the same as in (4), but the topic and comment roles are reversed:

6. The manager [topic; given] is PETE [comment; new].

It should be pointed out that this area is somewhat complex and the use of terms like *topic* is not consistent.

trajector and landmark These terms (introduced by Langacker) refer to profiled entities described as standing in a relationship, where one is more **salient** (the trajector) than the other (the landmark). Take the simple spatial relation expressed in *A is above B*. This is really 'about' A, which is the focus of attention (although both A and B are profiled): B functions only as a spatial reference point, and is relatively backgrounded. Here, A is the trajector and B the landmark. The terms can apply to any relationship, including, for instance, the subject (trajector) and object (landmark) of a transitive verb.

transition-relevance place   see under **conversational analysis**

transitive relations   see under **logical relations**

transitivity failures   It sometimes happens that a relation which in principle ought to be **transitive** (such as **meronymy** and **hyponymy**) appears in certain circumstances to lose its transitivity. One example involving hyponymy is the following:

1. A hang-glider is a type of glider.
2. A glider is a type of aeroplane.
3. ?A hang-glider is a type of aeroplane.

The reason for the transitivity failure in this case is that the class of things denoted by *glider* in the first line is not identical to the class denoted in the second line. Specifically, *glider* in line (2) denotes a narrower class (perhaps prototypical gliders) whose members ARE aeroplanes.

transitivity (grammatical)   see under **valency (of a verb)**

trial   A term in the **number system** of a few languages which denotes exactly three of whatever is being counted. It is quite rare, and only occurs as part of a four-term number system alongside **singular, dual,** and **plural**. One language with a trial is Marshallese, spoken in the Marshall Islands in the Pacific.

truth conditions   A **declarative** sentence as such does not have a **truth value**, but it can in principle be used to express **propositions** which will have truth values. However, a particular sentence, in literal use at least, cannot express just any proposition whatsoever: its propositional potential is limited by its **propositional content**. The conditions which must hold for a sentence to be usable to express a true proposition are known as its truth conditions. Among the conditions under which *The cat sat on the mat* can be used to express a true proposition, for instance, are the presence of a feline in an appropriate posture in contact with a floor covering of an appropriate type.

truth-conditional semantics   The basic tenet of a truth-conditional theory of meaning is that knowing the meaning of a sentence is equivalent to knowing the conditions under which it would express a true proposition. This approach deliberately imposes a restriction on what meaning phenomena are to count as 'semantics': only propositional meaning counts; non-propositional meaning is left for another discipline to deal with (for instance, 'pragmatics'). Part of the reason for this restriction is to make the subject matter easier to describe in terms of some system of formal logic.

truth values   In standard systems of logic, a truth value is a property of a **proposition**. There are normally only two possible truth values, namely 'true' and 'false'. Notice that a sentence like *The cat sat on the mat* does not have a truth value. It may, however, be used on a particular occasion to express a proposition, involving a particular cat and a particular mat, and this proposition will have a truth value. (Compare **truth conditions**.)

turn (conversational)   see under **conversational analysis**

type-token distinction   Consider the sentence *The cat sat on the mat*. How many words does it contain? The answer depends on whether we are talking about 'tokens' (that is, individual instances) or 'types': there are six word-tokens, but since two of the words are of the same type (the two occurrences of *the*), there are only five word-types. The use of a common noun to refer to a type rather than a token is quite frequent and often leads to potential ambiguity when a quantity is involved, as in the previous example.

U

ultimate scope of predication   see under **profile and base**

unaccusative verb   A type of intransitive verb (that is, a verb without a direct object), typically denoting a change of state or location, whose subject is not perceived as being actively involved in the action denoted by the verb. Typical examples are *die*, *fall*, *emerge*, *arrive*. In languages with a choice between (equivalents of) HAVE and BE as verbal auxiliaries, unaccusatives typically take BE: *Jean est/*a tombé/arrivé*. (Compare **unergative verbs**.)

understatement (also known as **litotes, meiosis**)   A figure of speech in which there is a statement of the quantity, intensity, or seriousness of something that is less than what is objectively the case, for rhetorical effect. (This definition excludes cases where there is an intention to misinform, as, for example, with casualty figures in a war situation.) The effect may be to de-emphasise something out of modesty, for example if a world-famous scientist acknowledges having 'made a small contribution to knowledge'. More often, perhaps, it is a form of **irony**, where the intention is to emphasise the opposite, as when a lottery winner of five million pounds is described as having acquired a 'tidy little nest-egg' (meaning 'a very large sum'), or when the Footballer of the Year admits to having 'scored a few goals' (thereby drawing attention to the large number he has in fact scored).

unergative verb   A type of intransitive verb, whose grammatical subject is perceived as being actively responsible for the action denoted by the verb. Examples are *run*, *telephone*, *exercise*, *resign*, *complain*. In languages with a choice between (equivalents of) HAVE and BE as verbal auxiliaries, unergatives typically take HAVE: *Jean a/*est téléphoné/rouspété*. (Compare **unaccusative verbs**.)

unmarked term (of opposition)   see **markedness**

uptake   This is sometimes suggested as an essential feature of a fully successful **speech act**. It refers to the hearer's acceptance of the validity of the speech act. Take the case of a promise – *I'll do it tomorrow*. Suppose the speaker sincerely intends to put themself under an obligation to carry out the act. But suppose also the hearer, for one reason or another, refuses to accept that an obligation has been entered into. Is the promise still a fully-fledged one? Or what about a purported congratulation for an event that the recipient regards as an unfortunate one? This is an area of uncertainty and controversy.

use vs mention   A linguistic expression can be employed in a sentence simply to represent itself rather than to stand for something else. This is said to be *mention* rather than *use* of the expression. Hence, *Snow is white* is a use of the word *snow*, whereas *Snow has four letters* is a mention. Mentions are usually signalled typographically:

Snow has four letters.
'Madam I'm Adam' is a palindrome.

utterance meaning   see under **sentence meaning vs utterance meaning**

$\boxed{\text{V}}$

valency (of a verb)   The number of arguments a verb takes. This has both a syntactic and a semantic aspect. The syntactic valency of a verb is (roughly speaking) the number of arguments needed for a sentence to be grammatical. There are different ways of counting syntactic arguments, but most agree that obligatory elements count towards a verb's valency and optional elements which become **latent** when omitted. Verbs are traditionally classified as 'intransitive' (one argument, e.g. *sneeze* in *Liz sneezed*), 'transitive' (two arguments, e.g. *stroked* in *Liz stroked the cat*) and 'ditransitive' (three arguments, e.g. *gave* in *Liz gave Pete some money*). Notice that *Liz gave Pete* is ungrammatical, so a noun-phrase expressing what is given is obligatory. *Liz gave some money* is possible, but in this case the beneficiary must be recoverable from the context, that is, it is latent and so is counted as part of the verb's valency. Semantic valency is the number of arguments for intuitive 'semantic completeness'. In the above cases, semantic intuition accords with a syntactic diagnosis. But while there is a broad correlation between these two, there are also some discrepancies. In some cases, the syntactic valency is greater than the semantic valency. For instance, it is usually considered that the subject *it* in a sentence like *It is raining* is semantically superfluous – it is a 'dummy subject', present only to satisfy the grammatical requirement that an English sentence must have a subject. Another example is the so-called 'cognate object' in *Liz smiled a wry smile*, which does not represent a second participant. In other cases, semantic valency outstrips syntactic valency, as in *The antique chair fetched an excellent price*. Here, we know that the event described includes a buyer and a seller, but there is no grammatical way of incorporating these into the inner structure of the sentence (without changing the verb).

vantage point   see **viewpoint**

variable   An element in a logical formula that can take any of a range of values. For instance, in the formula tall(x), 'x' is a variable which can take various values, yielding propositions such as tall(Pete) ('Pete is tall') or tall(the tree) ('The tree is tall'). For a logical formula to express a **proposition**, any variables it contains must be 'bound' by a **quantifier** (or be assigned a value, that is, be substituted by a constant). Thus $\forall x[man(x) \Rightarrow tall(x)]$ corresponds to 'Every man is tall', and $\exists x\ tall(x)$ corresponds to 'Something or someone is tall'. A variable that is not bound is called a 'free variable'.

vehicle   see under **tenor, vehicle and ground**

verification speed   see under **prototype effects**

viewpoint (vantage point)   The way something is described can depend on the position of the speaker relative to the thing being described. This is clearest in the case of spatial relations between objects. Take the case of a box next to a tree. Depending on the position of the speaker, this relationship can be (correctly) specified in a number of ways: *The box is in front of the tree, The box is behind the tree, The box is to the left of the tree, The box is to the right of the tree.*

voice   A morphological category of the verb which governs the relation between subject status and **functional role**. In the **active voice**, the subject is typically the 'most active' participant (see under **grammatical meaning** (3)); in the **passive voice**, the subject is typically the least active participant. Changing the voice of a transitive sentence does not change its **truth conditions**, but does change what the sentence 'is about':

Pete painted this picture.
This picture was painted by Pete.

There is also a 'middle voice', as in *The vase broke*, where an event involving a patient or theme is construed in such a way that the **agent** is ignored.

W

word   Exactly what constitutes a word differs from language to language, and even within a single language watertight definitions are hard to come by. Furthermore, different characterisations are needed for phonological words, syntactic words, and lexical items (which usually include **non-compositional** phrases such as **idioms**). For present purposes, we can say that a prototypical word has the following properties:

1. It is the smallest grammatical unit that can be moved around in a sentence or be separated from its fellows by the insertion of new material.
2. It is the largest unit which cannot be interrupted and whose elements cannot be reordered.
3. It consists of a single root, either alone or with one or more **affixes**.

word associations   There are two distinct understandings of the notion of word association, one psychological and the other text-based. Both have been proposed as offering insights into the nature of word meanings. The basic idea in both approaches is that the meaning of a word can be pictured as a network of connections with other words. The psychological approach draws on two main types of data. The first is the so-called 'free association' task, where subjects are given a word and have to respond with the first word that comes into their heads. The second type of data comes from observations of naturally occurring speech errors, where a 'wrong' word is substituted for an intended word. The idea is that both types of data will give information about the organisation of the **mental lexicon**. Results reveal five main types of relation between stimulus word and response word, and between intended word and produced word:

1. Co-hyponyms: (*red: blue, oil: vinegar, beer: wine, cat: dog.*
2. Opposites: (*heavy: light, fast: slow, hot: cold, black: white*)

((1) and (2) are sometimes grouped together as 'co-ordinates')

3. Collocates: (*front: door, big: brother, utter: nonsense*)

(Some cases, such as *black: blue* and *salt: pepper*, could be classified under either (1) or (3))

4. Superordinates: (*ant: insect, robin: bird, green: colour*)
5. Synonyms: (*sick: ill, begin: start, murder: kill*)

The text-based approach looks at the tendency of words to occur in close proximity in texts, and conclusions are drawn from the observed collocational patterns. Typically, different relationships are not distinguished.

Very large collections of texts (called 'corpuses' or 'corpora') can nowadays be analysed automatically.

X

X-questions   see under **interrogative**

Y

Yes-No questions   see under **interrogative**

Z

zero anaphora   see under **anaphora**

zero morph   This expression is used in two main ways:

1. To describe a case where the absence of an element carries information. For instance, the absence of the plural -s on *cow* indicates that it is singular. (Some scholars restrict the term to cases where some words have a non-zero mark for the meaning in question.)
2. To describe a case where most words in a class carry a mark, but in some cases it is absent, as with the plural of *sheep* (*Two cows/dogs/horses* vs *two sheep*). Notice that the absence of a mark on *sheep* does not of itself carry information regarding number.

zeugma   A type of semantic **anomaly** (it is also sometimes known as sortal crossing or, especially when deliberate, syllepsis). It occurs when a single occurrence of an expression has to be interpreted in two distinct ways simultaneously, as in *She was wearing a charming smile* *and a pair of slippers, He could well expire before his passport does.* The possibility of zeugma is one of a number of criteria for the diagnosis of the distinctness of **lexical senses,** and hence of **ambiguity.**

Bibliography

Works cited by author's name only in the text

Austin, J. L. (1962, 2nd rev. edn 1975), *How To Do Things With Words*, Oxford: Clarendon Press.

Chomsky, Noam (1965), *Aspects of the Theory of Syntax*, Cambridge, MA: MIT Press.

Fauconnier, Gilles (1994), *Mental Spaces* (2nd edn), Cambridge: Cambridge University Press.

Frawley, William (1992), *Linguistic Semantics*, Hillsdale, NJ: Lawrence Erlbaum Associates.

Grice, H. Paul (1989), *Studies in the Ways of Words*, Cambridge, MA: Harvard University Press.

Jackendoff, Ray (1990), *Semantic Structures*, Cambridge, MA: MIT Press.

Lakoff, George (1987), *Women, Fire and Dangerous Things*, Chicago: Chicago University Press.

Langacker, Ronald W. (1987), *Foundations of Cognitive Grammar*, vol. 1: *Theoretical Prerequisites*, Stanford, CA: Stanford University Press.

Langacker, Ronald W. (1991), *Foundations of Cognitive Grammar*, vol. 2: *Descriptive Application*, Stanford, CA: Stanford University Press.

Leech, Geoffrey, N. (1983), *Principles of Pragmatics*, London: Longman.

Pustejovsky, James (1995), *The Generative Lexicon*, Cambridge, MA: MIT Press.

Saussure, Ferdinand de (1916), *Cours de Linguistique Générale*, ed. Charles Bally and Albert Séchehaye, Paris: Payot.

Wierzbicka, Anna (1996), *Semantics: Primes and Universals*, Oxford: Oxford University Press.

Wittgenstein, Ludwig (1953), *Philosophical Investigations*, Oxford: Blackwell.

Recommended reading

1. General works on semantics and/or pragmatics

Introductory works

Cruse, D. A. (2004) *Meaning in Language: An Introduction to Semantics and Pragmatics* (2nd edn), Oxford: Oxford University Press. This is aimed at second year students, but it assumes no prior knowledge, and should not present difficulties to anyone familiar with the present volume. Has a descriptive, rather than a formal, bias. Provides exercises and suggested answers.

Grundy, Peter (2000) *Doing Pragmatics*, London: Arnold. A good, accessible introduction to all the main topics in pragmatics. Richly exemplified and with exercises.

Jaszczolt, Katarszyna (2002) *Semantics, Pragmatics and Beyond: Meaning in Language and Discourse*, London: Longman. Covers a wide range of topics in semantics and pragmatics. Aimed at undergraduates.

Kearns, Kate (2000) *Semantics*, Basingstoke and London: Macmillan. Clearly written. Strongly biased towards formal treatments (especially Montague semantics and possible world theory) and grammatical semantics, but has a chapter on implicatures. Provides exercises but no answers.

Lyons, J. (1995) *Linguistic Semantics: An Introduction*, Cambridge: Cambridge University Press. Although this is an introductory text, it is perhaps a little difficult for beginning undergraduates. It is, however, particularly good on the philosophical underpinnings of linguistic semantics. Short on concrete examples. No exercises.

Mey, Jacob (2001) *Pragmatics: An Introduction*, Oxford: Blackwell. Takes a broad view of pragmatics, going beyond what is covered in this Glossary.

Saeed, J. I. (1997) *Semantics*, Oxford: Blackwell. A good, accessible introduction to most of the main topics in semantics and pragmatics. Provides exercises but no answers.

Thomas, Jenny A. (1995) *Meaning in Interaction: An Introduction to Pragmatics*, London: Longman. Aimed at readers with no prior knowledge. Thorough explanation of basic concepts.

Verscheuren, Jef (1999) *Understanding Pragmatics*, London: Arnold. A good overview of the field. More difficult than Grundy or Thomas and more suitable for more advanced students. No exercises, but research topics are suggested.

More advanced general works

Allan, Keith (2001) *Natural Language Semantics*, Oxford and Malden, MA: Oxford University Press. Impressive coverage. Has a formalist bias, but still manages to include significant descriptive detail. Suitable for more advanced students. Includes questions for discussion, but no suggested answers.

Levinson, S. C. (1983) *Pragmatics*, Cambridge: Cambridge University Press. The first comprehensive overview of pragmatics as seen by a linguist.

Lyons, John (1977) *Semantics* (2 vols), Cambridge: Cambridge University Press. A classic text, covering most topics. Good discussion of structural semantics.

2. Books on more specialised topics (some necessarily more advanced)

Lexical semantics

Cruse, D. A. (1986) *Lexical Semantics*, Cambridge: Cambridge University Press. Covers a range of topics, including a detailed discussion of sense relations. (A more recent treatment of sense relations can be found in Croft and Cruse, see below.)

Murphy, M. Lynne (2003) *Semantic Relations and the Lexicon: Antonymy, Synonymy and Other Paradigms*, Cambridge: Cambridge University Press. A detailed discussion of sense relations and their relevance to the mental lexicon.

Formal semantics

Cann, Ronnie (1993) *Formal Semantics: An Introduction*, Cambridge: Cambridge University Press. Although an 'introduction', this is quite hard going and is not for beginners. However, anyone serious about engaging with formal semantics must not expect an easy ride. This book covers the basic ground, including Montague semantics, thoroughly and clearly.

Semantics in cognitive linguistics

Croft, William and Alan D. Cruse (2004) *Cognitive Linguistics*,

Cambridge: Cambridge University Press. This is the most recent general overview of cognitive linguistics. It contains substantial coverage of semantics.

Fauconnier, Gilles and Mark Turner (2002) *The Way We Think: Conceptual Blending and the Mind's Hidden Complexities*, New York: Basic Books. A lively and accessible introduction to conceptual blending and mental spaces.

Lakoff, George (1987) *Women, Fire and Dangerous Things*, Chicago: Chicago University Press. One of the foundation texts of cognitive linguistics. See particularly for conceptual categories and Conceptual Metaphor Theory.

Langacker, Ronald W. (1981) *Concept, Image and Symbol*, Berlin and New York: Mouton De Gruyter. An accessible introduction to most of Langacker's basic ideas.

Tsohadzidis, Savas L. (ed.) (1990) *Meanings and Prototypes: Studies in Linguistic Categorization*, London: Routledge. A useful collection of articles on prototype theory from various theoretical perspectives.

Grammatical semantics

Frawley, William (1992) *Linguistic Semantics*, Hillsdale, NJ: Lawrence Erlbaum Associates. The most complete account so far of grammatical semantics. Draws on data from a huge range of languages.

Componential approaches to semantics

Goddard, Cliff (1998) *Semantic Analysis: A Practical Introduction*, Oxford: Oxford University Press. An accessible introduction to Natural Semantic Metalanguage.

Jackendoff, Ray (1990) *Semantic Structures*, Cambridge, MA: MIT Press. Jackendoff is one of the two main current exponents of componential semantics in generative grammar (the other is Pustejovsky). This gives a clear exposition of his 'conceptual semantics'.

Pragmatics

Carston, Robyn (2002) *Thoughts and Utterances: The Pragmatics of Explicit Communication*, Oxford: Oxford University Press. The most up-to-date account of Relevance Theory. More readable than Sperber and Wilson.

Leech, Geoffrey N. (1983) *Principles of Pragmatics*, London: Longman. An idiosyncratic approach to pragmatics, but illuminating on politeness.

Levinson, S. C. (2000) *Presumptive Meanings*, Cambridge, MA: MIT Press. A more specialised and up-to-date treatment of conversational implicatures, presenting an alternative to Relevance Theory.

Searle, John R. (1969) *Speech Acts: An Essay in the Philosophy of Language*, Cambridge and New York: Cambridge University Press. An influential work on speech acts.

Sperber, Dan and Deirdre Wilson (1986) *Relevance: Communication and Cognition*, Oxford: Basil Blackwell. The foundational text of Relevance Theory.